WHAT CAN I DO?

WHAT CAN I DO?

MAKING A GLOBAL DIFFERENCE RIGHT WHERE YOU ARE

DAVID LIVERMORE

ZONDERVAN.com/
AUTHORTRACKER
follow your favorite authors

ZONDERVAN

What Can I Do?

This title is also available as a Zondervan ebook.
Visit www.zondervan.com/ebooks.

This title is also available in a Zondervan audio edition.
Visit www.zondervan.fm.

Requests for information should be addressed to:

Zondervan, *Grand Rapids, Michigan 49530*

Library of Congress Cataloging-in-Publication Data

Livermore, David A., 1967-
What can I do? : making a global difference right where you are / David Livermore.
p. cm.
Includes bibliographical references (p. 195).
ISBN 978-0-310-32596-3 (softcover)
1. Christian life. 2. Church and social problems. 3. Globalization—Religious aspects—Christianity. I. Title.
BV4509.5.L58 2011
248—dc22 2010034989

Cover design: Micha Kandros Design
Interior design: Matthew VanZomeren

Printed in the United States of America

---

11 12 13 14 15 /DCI/ 20 19 18 17 16 15 14 13 12 11 10 9 8 7 6 5 4 3 2 1

For Grace and Emily
I love you more!

CONTENTS

ACKNOWLEDGMENTS

I never used to read the acknowledgment pages in books, until I started writing myself. Now I better appreciate that no good book is possible without the collective efforts of many people. I wouldn't even know how to go about doing something like this alone. The people who have played a role in this project far exceed those I can list here, but I do need to name a few:

First, my thanks goes to the many individuals who allowed me to share a brief snapshot of their lives as compelling examples of what it means to live as we were created to live. Without their stories, this book would have remained a bunch of abstract ideas. More important, I'm thankful for how they inspire me to make a difference in the world.

Second, I want to say a particular word of thanks to my former student Julie Slagter. Julie was especially instrumental in helping me gather the many stories, ideas, and research gathered for part 2 of the book. If Julie had her way, every page would have included an example of human trafficking, because that's the cause that's captured her heart and life. This is a better book because she joined me in the rigorous work of pulling it together and worked with me on some of the earliest drafts.

Next, thank you to the friends and colleagues I subjected to a really rough version of this manuscript. Steve Argue, Jeanette Banashak, Rob Bell, Dave Horne, Marsha Johnson, Grace Man, Steve Mayer, Graham McKeague, and Julie Slagter made this a much better finished product.

Thanks to Ryan Pazdur, my editor at Zondervan, for sharing my enthusiasm for communicating this message and for the many value-added suggestions and gracious critiques along the way.

And to Linda, Emily, and Grace: There's little that matters to me in life that isn't connected to you. You've endured another round of my obsessing about what to include, what to leave out, how to say it, and when to squeeze in the time to get it all done. More than that, I love that together we're on our own adventure to make the world a better place, one day at a time.

FOREWORD

There's a reason why Dave's book is so important.

But first, a story.

There is a legendary rabbinic tale about a rabbi from Cracow. He has a dream in which he sees that there is great treasure buried under a bridge in a far-off city. When he wakes up, he decides to journey to that far-off city to get the treasure that he's seen in his dream. He arrives at the bridge only to discover that it's guarded by police, and so he hides in the bushes, trying to figure out how to get the treasure.

One of the guards sees him and says, "You there! What are you doing?"

The rabbi steps out of the bushes and says, "Well, I had this dream in which I saw treasure under this bridge ..."

The policeman laughs. "You believe in dreams like that? If I did, then I would believe in the dream that I had, that there's treasure buried under the bed of some rabbi in Cracow."

The rabbi thanks the policeman and races home.

So what does that story have to do with this book?

Dave writes here about a life that is right in our own backyard. He's not saying that the action is somewhere else, with someone else. He's not telling you to quit your job and move to Africa if you want to really live. He's not teaching that you need more resources so that you can really make a difference. He's writing in this book about how each of us can turn the tide from exactly where we are.

This is a powerful truth we need now more than ever.

What I so deeply appreciate about Dave is how wide open his eyes are. He sees possibility and potential all over the place. Every time I hear him speak, I am inspired by what's right in front of me.

But this book isn't just inspiring; this book is as practical as it gets. Business, art, justice, education — Dave shows us what daily engagement with the great causes of our time looks like, wherever we find ourselves.

He helps us wake up, as if from a dream, discovering that what we've been looking for is not under a bridge in a far-off city.

It's been here, the whole time.

—*Rob Bell*

INTRODUCTION

Yes, you. The one who thinks it's Bono's job to save the world.

Yes, you. The one trapped in cubicle world who goes to church, hears about all the great things *others* are doing, and feels even more disconnected.

Yes, you. The one who has no desire to hop on a plane or learn a foreign language.

Yes, you. The one who would love to hop on a plane but can't see how that really meets the world's greatest needs.

Yes, you. The one who just picked up this book to read. God is inviting you to be part of making the world a better place. And now you're going to read about all sorts of people just like you doing their part.

My wife, Linda, and I often discuss what it means for us to make a difference in the world. More and more, our daughters, Emily and Grace, join the conversations with us. But we often have moments when it's hard to see beyond the immediate stresses of our own fast-paced lives.

One night after the girls went to bed, Linda and I got ready to watch the movie we had rented. We had heard so much about *Hotel Rwanda*, a visceral account of the Rwandan genocide, and at last we had a chance to watch it. We made the popcorn, closed the blinds, and got comfortable. Two hours later, the credits were rolling, the popcorn remained untouched, and we sat in silence. We didn't know whether to feel enraged, numb, guilty, or inspired by what we had just watched.

A guy like me *should* know what to do. I've spent the night in villages along the Amazon, Nile, and Pearl rivers. I've visited the killing fields in Cambodia, former concentration camps in Europe, and refugee camps in Sierra Leone and Ethiopia. I'm in Africa and Asia almost as much as I'm home in Grand Rapids, Michigan. My work is devoted to helping leaders see and effectively engage with global issues. But for some reason, I was unusually paralyzed sitting in my own living room after watching Don Cheadle's compelling portrayal of Paul Rusesabagina, the hotel owner who stayed behind to save as many as possible. I sat there thinking, *The Rwanda genocide is over, but this same thing is going on right now in many other places. But what can we possibly do about it?* My head hurt, and part of me just wanted to crawl into bed and move on with the assembly line of life. But I couldn't. Slowly Linda and I started to process it together. For the next several days, we deliberated the implications for us and for our relatively comfortable existence as a family.

I rarely encounter someone who doesn't give a rip when faced with the reality of life for the poor and oppressed. Most people I know feel an urge to do something when they hear about the high death rates among kids in Sub-Saharan Africa, see a documentary on women trafficked for sex in Southeast Asia, or watch news reports about people running for their lives in war-torn regions. But many of us don't have a clue what we can really do about it.

The atrocities continue right this minute. Tribes are feuding, suicide bombers are plotting, and people are dying. There's something desperately amiss in the world. But if all we do is keep talking about the problems, it's too reminiscent of our parents telling us to finish our dinner because there are children starving in other parts of the world. Most of us were willing to FedEx our leftovers to anyone who would take them. But somehow we knew that wouldn't make any difference. And what can we do about enslaved children, dirty water, and entire cultural groups who have never encountered Jesus?

Actually—quite a bit!

• • •

I've organized this book into three parts. Part 1 starts with the big picture. The first chapter describes the global issues facing our generation, and the second one looks at the invitation to join God in redeeming the world. Chapter 3 offers some immediate big-picture strategies for making a difference today.

Part 2 has several chapters of stories and ideas about people in lots of different professions and fields who are serving globally. A few of these examples involve people traveling overseas, but most of these stories take place closer to home. You'll meet business leaders grappling with the ethics of globalization in a way that neither provides simplistic answers nor shrugs off exploiting the poor to the advantage of the rich. You'll learn from schoolteachers, aunts, uncles, parents, and siblings influencing kids to improve life for more people on the planet. I'll introduce you to scientists doing innovative research to discover solutions to malaria, HIV/AIDS, and global warming. And you'll encounter filmmakers, performers, and composers creating art that exposes us to the issues, concerns, and causes of our day. The stories in this section come from people I've encountered along the way and from data gathered in the Glocal Service Project—research which examined ways North Americans invest in local and global activism from home. Most of the stories were gathered through focus groups and interviews. Part 2 ends with a few cautions that, when heeded, will improve your effectiveness in making a global difference.

Part 3 will guide you into the next steps of this journey. I've included a discernment process in chapter 10 to help you identify ways to get involved, and chapter 11 helps you do this with a group (families, small groups, churches, and so on). The appendix includes some frequently asked questions (FAQs) you might want to peek at now (or anytime along the way).

• • •

I realize your life isn't exactly a cakewalk. We all have our share of problems and struggles. But for most of us, our personal problems pale in comparison with worldwide tragedies like poverty, civil war, and disease. Yet they weigh on us just the same. Whether it's figuring out how to make the next mortgage payment, caring for our aging parents, deciding where to go to college, or (fill in the blank), our lives are not exactly picture perfect.

Yet we know we can't just shrug off the needs of the world and go on with life. The causes are too important and the situations too tragic. Join me to learn how you can orient your interests, skills, and relationships to meet some of the most pressing needs of our day. God is ready to use you to make a global difference in the world—right where you are!

PART 1

A BIG (INSPIRING YET OVERWHELMING) PICTURE

Real change happens as each of us chooses to make a difference right where we are — in our neighborhoods, factories, classrooms, offices, and homes. But if we begin by plotting strategies to make the world a better place without first seeing and understanding the big picture of God's purposes, we will inevitably end up disoriented and burned out. So let's begin with a thirty-thousand-foot view of the world.

Our aerial perspective begins above a hypothetical "global village." This kind of big-picture perspective on the differences and similarities between people is necessary to inform a thoughtful and nuanced response to the problems and challenges we face today. After looking at the world, we'll take a wide-angled view of the Scriptures — from Genesis to Revelation — to hear God's repeated invitation to make our world a better place. And we'll conclude this section with some big ideas about how we can make a difference — starting today.

CHAPTER 1

WELCOME TO THE NEIGHBORHOOD

YOUR GLOBAL VILLAGE

Imagine you've just moved to a town of one thousand people. It's an unusual place because it's been designed as a microcosm of the world. The ethnic and economic diversity across the globe can be seen and experienced right here in your new community. Disease, literacy rates, and access to things like electricity and water are all present in this village. It's as if the worldwide population of 6.7 billion people has suddenly shrunk to this single town of a thousand people. Now that you've moved here, you have a unique opportunity to see what life is like for people all over the world.

At first it might feel like you've moved to Chinatown, because 600 of the 1,000 community members are from Asia, most of them of Chinese descent. Another 140 are from Africa, 120 from Europe, 80 from Latin America, 50 from the United States and Canada, and 10 from the South Pacific, including places like Australia and New Zealand (see figure on p. 20).

World Population by Region

Unicef, "The State of the World's Children 2009," *www.unicef.org/sowc09/report/report.php* (April 28, 2010).

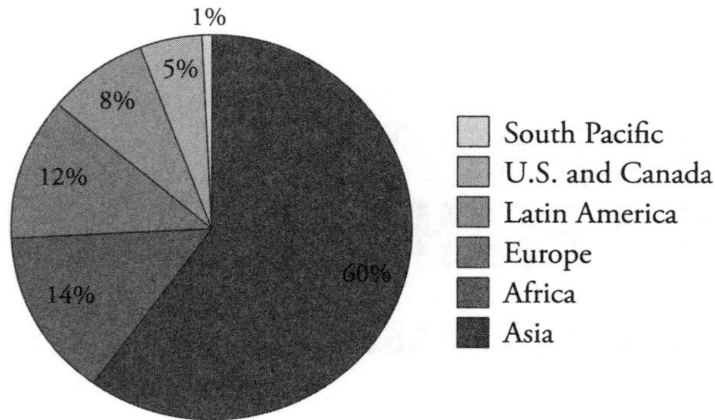

There are 510 males and 490 females. Sadly, girls are more likely to be aborted than boys in places like India and China because of the "noble" honor of having a son in these cultures, particularly if you're allowed only one child.

- 330 kids under the age of eighteen live in this global village, half of whom have received immunizations against preventable diseases like measles and polio.
- 20 new babies are born every year here, so the town is growing. One of these babies will die before his or her first birthday.
- 9 people die every year, 3 from hunger and 1 from cancer.
- 60 senior citizens (age sixty-five and older) live in the village.
- 500 people are malnourished. If you have adequate food and nutrients, chances are your neighbors on either side do not. That's the way it is — fifty-fifty. One person has proper nourishment; one doesn't.
- 800 of the people in this town live in substandard housing.
- 670 people can't read. If you're reading these words, you're obviously among the privileged minority.
- 330 are without access to a safe water supply.

- 240 don't have any electricity. Of the 760 town members who do have electricity, most are able to use it for only a couple hours at night.
- Only 70 people have access to the internet. Social networking, email, and the World Wide Web aren't the answer to everything. Only 7 percent of the world has access to them. That number grows daily, but we still have a long way to go.
- 10 people, 1 percent of the world, have a college education.
- 10 individuals have HIV/AIDS, and most of them are women and children.
- 400 people have never heard of Jesus. Forty percent of the people in your new town don't have a clue who Jesus is.
- The town has 5 soldiers, 7 teachers, and 1 doctor. The doctor keeps pretty busy but primarily treats those who can afford to pay. The 7 teachers have their hands full, although 25 percent of the kids go to work every day instead of school.

One hundred people, 10 percent of the population, control enough explosive power in nuclear weapons that they could blow up the entire civilization many times over. The other 900 people watch with deep anxiety, wondering if the 100 can get along well enough to avoid using the weapons. These 900 wonder if the ones who control the weapons might inadvertently set them off. Or if they ever decide to dismantle the weapons, where in town will they dispose of the dangerous radioactive materials used to make them? The newspaper in town never seems to include this perspective, however.[1]

The only part of this scenario that doesn't exist in real life is the actual 1,000-member village. But if you were to expand the population of this imaginary village to 6.7 billion people, all of the above realities and proportions would apply. This *is* the village where we live. These *are* the issues facing us. These are the inequities of life in the twenty-first-century world. We no longer have the luxury of viewing the wants and needs of our family and community apart from those living in the rest of the world. The shoes we wear, the food we eat, and the companies we work for are all intertwined with our fellow village members scattered across the globe.

Far too many books and documentaries stop here. We read the alarming disparities with little guidance about how to respond. I've promised you a more solution-oriented, hopeful picture, and I assure you — the rest of this book is oriented that way. But before we respond, it's helpful to understand seven of the most important realities facing our neighborhood. Let's start with the first one — money.

ECONOMIC IMBALANCE

Back in our 1,000-member village, there are 5 *extremely* wealthy people who control most of the money. And 200 town members, one-fifth of the village, own 74 percent of all the financial assets.

Imagine how different your life is if you are privileged to be among the top 20 percent. Those in the top 20 percent of the village live on about seventy dollars a day, while those in the bottom 20 percent live on about one dollar a day. If you're among the bottom 20 percent, or even among the majority in the middle, you'll need to think creatively about how to feed your loved ones today. You are largely dependent on the generosity of your wealthier neighbors.

Keep in mind that these are more than numbers and statistics. The implications of these numbers can be very personal when you begin meeting people from other parts of the world. The first time I taught a weeklong course in Liberia, a small coastal country in West Africa, I asked my host when we should break for lunch. He hesitated before responding, and then he said, "Well, most of us eat only one meal a day. While we're in class today, our spouses and children will work to earn some money by selling things like rice, water, and vegetables. Hopefully, they'll get enough money for us to have a small meal together tonight when we get home." Then he looked at me and said, "But feel free to eat your lunch whenever you wish. I'd be happy to take you somewhere." Needless to say, I lost my appetite and decided I could easily go without lunch for a week. I spend my life talking with people about these issues and helping them see how their lives compare with the lives of others, but I'm still caught off guard by the chasm between my economic realities and those of so many other people.

The economic issues of our day are further complicated by globalization, the expansion and integration of international manufacturing and business. Stop reading for a moment and look at the label on your clothes or shoes. Where were they made? The shirt I'm wearing says, "Made in Bangladesh." While I sit in the comfort of my home, it's hard for me to envision the worn faces of the people whose hands fed this fabric through the industrial sewing machines in Dhaka. I'm rarely conscious of the tired crew on the cargo ship that transported my shirt across the ocean, nor do I think about the fatigued customs official who got involved in the shipment. What truck drivers spent time away from home to deliver this shirt to the big-box store where a second-shift worker neatly folded it on a shelf for me to buy? But these people are my neighbors in our global village. I'm repulsed at the thought that my shirt might have been made by a child who works in a factory in Bangladesh rather than attending school.

Before we go too far down the path of offering pat answers or simplistic solutions, let's agree that there are *no easy answers* to most of these issues. I've promised a more solution-focused response, and we'll get there. But for the time being, we're simply trying to get a glimpse of the needs in our village. If you want another, more personalized perspective on all this, take a moment to check out your economic place at *www.globalrichlist.com*. You may be surprised to learn that someone who earns fifty thousand dollars a year is among the top 1 percent of the richest people in the global village! Maybe you're a recent high school or college grad making only twenty thousand dollars a year? You're still in the top 11 percent. The economic disparity between the rich and the poor, and even between the middle class and the poor, is often bigger than we think. It's an issue that demands the attention of consumers, business leaders, economists, and leaders in the church. Our response to these dilemmas will often be misguided if we fail to get our bearings and grasp some of these larger global concerns. The massive economic imbalance we see in our world today is one of the most challenging and ghastly realities facing us in the twenty-first century.

DISEASE AND OUR GLOBAL HEALTH

Many of the same people struggling to survive on a dollar a day are also the ones most susceptible to fatal diseases. While life expectancy has been going up for most people in our global village, HIV/AIDS and malaria continue to reverse that trend, particularly for our neighbors from Southern Africa, parts of Southeast Asia, Latin America, and certain pockets within Russia.

In Sub-Saharan Africa, for example, HIV/AIDS is the leading cause of death. Most *victims* of HIV/AIDS globally are women and children, not promiscuous men.[2] It is estimated that in certain tribal groups in Southwest China, half the population is infected with HIV/AIDS, and this percentage may be even higher in reality. In India, many Punjabi truck drivers sleep with different women all the way up and down the country during their monthlong journeys, infecting each woman they meet along the way, as well as their unsuspecting wives once they're back home with the family.

Or how about malaria? For me, a mosquito bite is usually a mere annoyance. But for many people in our village, a mosquito bite easily leads to malaria. At "best," getting malaria means experiencing an awful case of the flu, including a high fever and chills. Left untreated, it frequently leads to death. Nearly one million people in the world die from malaria every year, mostly young children. There *are* cures for malaria. These children could be spared by simply getting them the right medicine.

But there's an epidemic killing even more people worldwide than either HIV/AIDS or malaria. In fact, this disease kills more adults in our global village than all other infectious diseases combined. Nearly half the world's refugees are infected with it. It's an ancient disease that was nearly wiped out a generation ago, but it's back today with a raging force—tuberculosis. Look around your town of 1,000 people. Three hundred and thirty people, nearly one-third of the world's population, have TB.[3]

These diseases are not limited to the developing world. They're also found in places like the United States, France, and Singapore. But the highest fatality rates are in the developing world. What can we do so that malaria, TB, HIV/AIDS, heart disease, and cancer become history in our village? There are ways to lessen the impact of these diseases on our neighbors. We'll get there.

ENVIRONMENT AND OUR NEIGHBORS

It's an embarrassment that Christians have often spent so much energy mocking "tree huggers" and generally downplaying their responsibility to be faithful stewards of the environment. Now, I'm well aware that a great deal of controversy remains over the issue of global warming and the degree to which our behavior can change this effect. But the Bible is clear about our responsibility to care for this planet. From the very beginning of time, part of what it meant to be made in God's image was to be a caretaker of the animals and our planet.

Six billion tons of trash end up in the sea every year. Take a walk along any beach in the world, and you'll find washed-up bottles, lighters, plastic bags, toothbrushes, and more. Much of the diverse animal and plant life on our planet lives in the sea, and many of the people who live in our global village rely on fish for a large part of their daily food source. When we pollute the water in our rivers and oceans, we pollute the fish. And when we pollute the fish, we put our neighbors at risk.

There are similar connections between the issues of climate change, energy use, and water consumption. Many of us have never really considered the degree to which our oil-dependent lifestyle affects the lives of people in Mozambique and Myanmar, by influencing the changing sea levels and increasing the susceptibility these people have to tropical diseases. We're in desperate need of Christian scientists, politicians, and consumers who can wrestle with environmental issues and offer us sustainable ways to address them. The best way for you to help your neighbors in the global village might be from a laboratory in rural Illinois or by organizing a recycling program.

TRAFFICKING AND GLOBAL LUST

From street-level dealers to multinational empires that rival governments in size, the drug-trafficking business is the largest organized crime ring in our global community. Greed, power, and the need for a quick fix are what drive this worldwide industry. Places like the "Golden Triangle," a relatively lawless region at the intersection of Myanmar, Laos, and Thailand, are infamous for producing huge amounts of illicit opium. Drug use is rampant in the bourgeois, affluent suburbs of Chicago, Tucson, and Indianapolis. But make no mistake. There's a clear correlation between socioeconomic status and drug use. Economically depressed people are the ones most susceptible to drug use.

Second only to drug trafficking is human trafficking, a thirty-two-billion-dollar slave industry built on forcing people to do things against their will. At any given time, somewhere between thirteen million and twenty-seven million people in the world are being forced to perform acts against their will. Most of those living in slavery are kids.[4] Some of the kids in your village are being held in slavery instead of going to school every day. They're often abducted from their homes and forced to sell their bodies, fight in wars, and work night and day making bricks, tending land, and cleaning people's homes. You don't have to look very far around our global village to see the "winners" and losers of human trafficking.

On a recent trip to Liberia, I met Jimmy, a sixteen-year-old who loves school more than any teenager I know. But to understand his love for education, you first have to understand Jimmy's childhood. While some of his peers around the world went to Little League, Jimmy was aiming a machine gun at anyone who walked by. By the time he was eleven, he had lost count of how many people he had killed for the rebel army that had abducted and trained him. Then one day, a U.N. worker coaxed Jimmy's weapons from him in exchange for schoolbooks and an education. Estimates vary widely, but it's believed there are more than three hundred thousand child soldiers in the world. Boys like Jimmy, as young as six years old, are forced into local armies where they're trained as soldiers for guerrilla warfare. In addition, their forced military service usually involves providing sexual services to the men in the army.

Let's take a closer look at something as wonderful and seemingly innocent as chocolate. Thirty-five percent of the chocolate available for purchase in our village is made from cocoa beans harvested by slaves. In Côte d'Ivoire, the largest producer of cocoa beans in the world, young boys are subjected to extreme abuse and inhumane conditions while being forced to harvest the beans from which chocolate is made.[5]

The most prevalent form of trafficking is the coercion of women and children into the sex business. Some are lured into the trade through the promise of a good job in another country or through a false marriage proposal that turns into a bondage situation. Others are sold to a sex lord by their parents, husbands, or boyfriends, and many are kidnapped. Sex traffickers frequently subject their victims to a fictitious debt that never seems to be reduced no matter how many sexual services are performed. Victims endure starvation, confinement, physical abuse, gang rape, and threats of violence to their families and against them personally. Many of them are forced to take drugs. You can find these trafficked girls at a brothel in your village, but you might also find them at a nearby nail salon or the local truck stop.

The traffickers aren't the only ones who benefit from these abominable practices. Other beneficiaries include weapons manufacturers, chocolate sellers, the taxi drivers who drive customers to brothels, and fast-food restaurants that supply food to traffickers waiting for their "product" to be sold on a cold, dark street corner. In many situations, local police also make a profit from this trade by receiving bribes to look the other way. To a certain extent, you and I unconsciously "benefit" from many of these industries. Yet in another sense, we don't. Ultimately, no one benefits from a village that allows some of its members to be dehumanized, abused, and tortured for the sake of financial profit and personal pleasure. The number of people being trafficked is beginning to lessen because more people are standing up and saying, "Enough!" Much remains to be done, but some are hopeful we may see this atrocity eradicated in our lifetime.

WAR AND THE ABUSE OF POWER

What about war? The tragedy of war is ancient, but there's a new dynamic to war in the twenty-first century, one that includes weapons of mass destruction, terrorism, and suicide bombers. Among the many lessons that emerged from 9/11 is the reality that we live in a world where a small number of people can kill masses of people very quickly. Even first-rate intelligence services like those of the

U.S. government cannot ensure there won't be further attacks using airplanes, bombs, anthrax, chemical weapons, and dirty bombs.

To a large degree, a bigger battle between tribalism and globalism has replaced the battles we used to see between one nation and another. The great divisions of our day center on vastly different views about how life should be lived. Greed for money and power are still the primary driving forces in war, as they always have been. But there's an additional force now, where one civilization is enraged by the behavior of another. And more often than not, these different civilizations are now living next door to each other. The fault lines between worldviews and civilizations have become the battle lines of our time.

Western civilizations are appalled that a state religion like Islam can mandate how the two sexes relate to one another. Islamic fundamentalists are furious to see American military bases built on their religious sites. Europeans lobby against the Hindu caste system. Many Eastern civilizations are perplexed at the syncretistic mix of Western religion with consumerism. Christians and Muslims target each other's populations as evangelistic pursuits. Christians who fight for the freedom to pray in school simultaneously protest the freedom of Muslims to wear religious head coverings at work.

Even those individuals who never leave their local village or city are encountering the clash of civilizations through what they see on the internet or on television. Eighteen-year-old men in Islamabad watch Brittany Spears erotically gyrating with a cross hanging around her neck. Fifteen-year-olds in Nashville see their peers in Gaza tying bombs to their bodies out of loyalty to their religion.

How will we respond to the issue of war in our generation? Will our churches allow room for the expression of different political ideals while uniformly centering on the person and work of Jesus? It's hard to imagine a more poignant picture of our desperate need for hope and redemption than the global problem of war.

THE SHIFTING GLOBAL LANDSCAPE

Despite the endless news stories about the bursting emergence of China and India as key global powers, many still struggle to see beyond outdated characterizations of these ancient nation-states. I'm often surprised to hear people talk about China and India as backward, poverty-stricken behemoths. Many are inclined to think of China as Pearl Buck described it in her best-selling book *The Good Earth*: a farming society with struggling peasants, greedy landowners, famines, floods, plagues, and poverty. Say "India," and people often picture Dalits wading through mud in the slums of Calcutta. While there's still a kernel of truth in these stereotypes, they're extremely myopic perceptions of these rising tigers.

Over 200 of the 1,000 people in our imaginary village are from China. They may easily come from one of the twenty fastest growing cities in the world—all of which are in China. China's economy has grown over 9 percent a year for more than thirty years. During the last couple of decades, nearly five hundred million Chinese have moved from rural communities to cities and from poverty to middle class. India is rising right next door with a similar-sized population. Stand at the first tee of the KGA golf club in downtown Bangalore, and you can see the glimmering towers of IBM, Microsoft, and Goldman Sachs.[6] This is not your grandparents' India and China! Any responsible understanding of the twenty-first-century world must include an accurate, up-to-date understanding of the rising importance of China and India.

The statistics that come out of China simply boggle the mind. China is the world's largest producer of coal, steel, and cement. It's the biggest cell phone market in the world. Its exports to the United States have grown by 1,600 percent over the past fifteen years. China manufactures two-thirds of the world's photocopiers, microwave ovens, DVD players, and shoes.[7] Yes, there are still many peasant farmers in China. Many minority people *are* struggling to survive and are oppressed by several realities already covered in this chapter, including poverty, disease, and trafficking. No one knows exactly how China's emergence as a global superpower will play out over the next couple decades, but most leaders in economics, business, and political science agree that we're wise to pay attention.

Another 200 people in our village are from India. India's greatest resource is its human capital—a vast and growing population of entrepreneurs, managers, and business-savvy professionals.

Up-and-coming Indian professionals are buying lattes, iPods, washing machines, cars, and homes. India is the only country with a rate of consumption higher than that of the United States.[8] Unfortunately, the images of Dalits struggling in the slums are still just as much a part of India today. Even though the number of people in India's middle class now equals the amount of people in the entire United States—three hundred million—another seven hundred million Indians are living in desperate squalor.

India and China aren't the only emerging economies. Others are scattered across Central Europe, Africa, Asia, and Latin America. Brazil and Russia are often lumped in with China and India, forming the BRIC (Brazil, Russia, India, and China) economies. Many of us, particularly through our jobs, will continue to find ourselves dealing with the new opportunities these growing economies provide. Teachers, business executives, manufacturers, and medical professionals need to have a global, big-picture perspective to wisely respond in conversations and as they make decisions that relate to these emerging economies.

THE FAITHFUL

Finally, there's a surging revival of religious faith occurring around the world. Brazilians are conducting exorcisms, Nigerians are fighting over Islam and Christianity, and Chinese executives are leading house churches. Nations like Russia, Turkey, India, and the United States are led by people who are unabashedly religious.

Here's how the world worships in your 1,000-member neighborhood. There's one Catholic church, one Protestant, and one Orthodox congregation. There's also a mosque, a Hindu temple, and a Buddhist temple.

About one-third of the people in our global village call themselves Christians. One hundred ninety-nine are Catholic, 99 are Protestant, and 42 are Orthodox.

There are 184 Muslims, 137 Hindus, 64 Buddhists, and 56 Animists. The remaining 219 people living in your town follow a variety of religions, including Judaism and Taoism. A few in this group identify themselves as atheists.

As the world becomes more mobile and interconnected, Muslims, Jews, Christians, and Hindus are increasingly living alongside each other. Islam is growing at a rate of 2.7 percent annually, Hinduism at 2.2 percent, and Buddhism at 1.7 percent.[9]

These statistics, combined with the depressing events covered in the evening news (and even many missions reports) can feel overwhelming to some Christians. But the Christian faith is also growing, faster than ever before in world history, at a rate of 6.9 percent a year.[10] On average, two people surrender their lives to Jesus every second. Most of this growth is happening in Latin America, Southern Africa, and Southern Asia, but it's also evident in places like Iran and the United States.

At the same time, 400 people in your village have never encountered Jesus. They aren't antagonistic and militantly opposed to Christianity; they've just never had the chance to accept or reject Jesus and know almost nothing about him.

UNDERSTAND THE BIG PICTURE

There are several challenges we haven't begun to address here, including orphans, refugees, abortion, literacy, access to clean water, education, and many others. Many of these problems are interconnected. And it's important to remember that all is not gloom and despair in the world. Alongside the inequities, evil, and heartache, there's hope. Per capita incomes and literacy rates are rising in almost every country. Life expectancy worldwide is sixty-six years, a record high. Hunger is in retreat in many parts of the world, smog is down 30 percent since 1970 (even though there are twice as many cars on the road!), and crime is in significant decline. Everywhere we look, we see signs that God is at work, reversing the curse of evil and ushering the cosmos toward a new reality. In some places, we can see evidence of God's redemption unfolding right before our eyes. Without question, though, there's a great deal left for us to do. HIV/AIDS is challenging the improved life-expectancy rate, terrorism is infringing on human rights, and most significantly, many people continue to die without ever encountering Jesus.

The first step toward making a difference in the world is simply growing in our awareness of what's happening on our planet. Research demonstrates that *individuals who understand global issues and see themselves as global citizens most often feel a need to give back to society and work for the rights of others.*[11] It's difficult to orient our lives and our work around the needs of our neighbors if we don't know what they need. A growing understanding of life in our shrinking village can be one of the most powerful ways to inform how we can get involved.

The world is groaning for redemption. Fatherless children long to be loved. Trafficked women hope for freedom. Hungry families crave food. There's something desperately amiss in our world, but there's hope. A global perspective combined with your God-given interests, relationships, and experiences is a part of how Christ will redeem the world we share.

BEFORE YOU TURN THE PAGE

Review the issues presented in this chapter:

- Economic Imbalance
- Disease and Our Global Health
- Environment and Our Neighbors
- Trafficking and Global Lust
- War and the Abuse of Power
- The Shifting Global Landscape
- The Faithful

What reality strikes a nerve with you the most?

Ask God to use this book to help you integrate your life, work, and giftings with addressing this issue.

CHAPTER 2

YOU WERE MADE FOR THIS!

Sex slaves. AIDS babies. Broken families. Child soldiers. Diseased rivers. These words don't belong together. This is *not* how it was supposed to be. You were not created to live in a global neighborhood plagued with the inequities we just encountered.

You were made for a place where *everyone* enjoys: Everlasting worship. Perfect sex. Life-giving work. Healthy babies. Authentic relationships. This *is* how it was intended to be. And God invites us to join the work of making this a reality again — heaven on earth.

Mission types like me often default to "shaming" people into caring about global atrocities. My work puts me in a village church in Cambodia one weekend where the offering baskets are passed around three times in hopes there will be enough money to buy medicine to keep a church member's baby alive. The following week, I'm speaking at a megachurch in Midwest U.S.A., hearing appeals for the "must-have" ten-million-dollar building addition. Experiences like that can make me just a little bit nutty. So I confess that I've done my share of ranting and raving to American congregations about our need to wake up to the real needs of the world. If allowed a few minutes to share some pictures and tell some heart-wrenching stories, I can easily add a bit of realism to the typical middle-class perspective on life.

But more and more, I question what's gained by beating people up with a global chip on my shoulder. Surely, there are times we should feel guilty for the way we steward our resources. I'm deeply moved when I see a short-term missions participant transform from being calloused, insensitive, and self-absorbed to uncontrollably sobbing when confronted by kids living in a dump. But all too often, when we get back home to the machine of materialism, deadlines, and keeping up appearances, the tears and discomfort we experienced so profoundly become little more than a fading memory of good intentions. Think about it. Are there any commitments you've sustained long-term by guilt?

God invites us to make the world a better place. That's the primary reason for us to get involved globally. The urge to respond to the needs of our day taps directly into the core of our identity as human beings—God's image bearers. Since the beginning of time, God has been inviting us to partner in the divine work of creating and developing new things. This invitation is woven throughout the Scriptures, from Genesis to Revelation. To continue our big-picture view, we turn to see some of the epochal moments of God's story. This larger story helps us answer two of the most central questions in life: Who am I? And why am I here?

God's Invitation from Genesis to Revelation

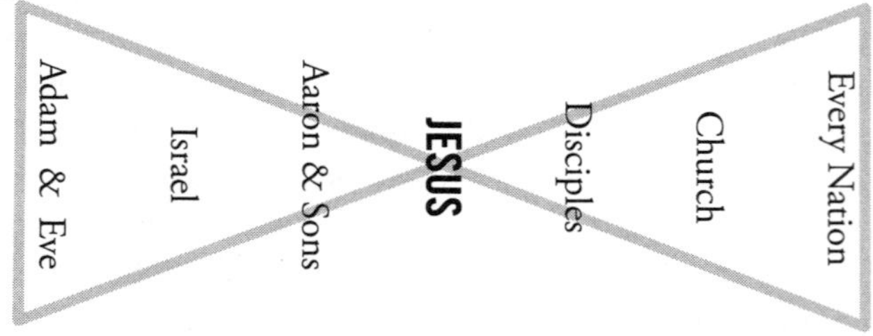

ADAM AND EVE (GENESIS 1–2)

To understand the origins of what we typically refer to as "mission," we have to go all the way back to Eden. Our story began with perfection. God created the world, looked at it, and said, "It's good. It's all very good." Everything God made declared the beauty and glory of our triune God. The heavens and earth were fully characterized by *shalom*—peace, wholeness, unity, harmony, and perfection. And God created the world with a generative energy, making a cosmos that is constantly changing and continuously bursting forward with new energy every second, every day. Creation never stops. The forests, gardens, and oceans are different today than they were yesterday. And life keeps lunging forward with every breath.[1]

Best of all, God created Adam and Eve as the pinnacle of creation. Unlike everything else, they were made in God's *image*. If you want to get a glimpse of what God looks like, look at the person next to you. As stewards of God's creation, invited to order, develop, and responsibly care for God's world, we are living pictures of God, albeit incomplete images of the divine. In a mysterious and wonderful way, we were made to be God's physical presence in the world. No higher honor could have been given to us.[2] This is who we are. This is why we're here.

Mission means *acting on God's behalf in the world and reflecting God's glory*. It's core to why we were made. It includes our calling to reign over creation, develop it, and direct its use to the glory of God.[3] Some scholars refer to this as a *priestly* role that was given to us as humanity. From the beginning of time, we were created to be intermediaries between God and the rest of creation—priests.[4]

Adam and Eve were God's primary way of caring for the animals and bringing divine order and creativity to the earth. Everything Adam and Eve did in the garden depended on them living as God's partners. And just about every job we pursue today also involves being a coworker with God in the world. Data processing, plumbing, web design, politics, engineering, art, garbage collection, newspaper reporting, town planning, retail work, landscape gardening, lab technology, and preaching and equipping the saints (Eph. 4:11–12) are all roles connected to our missional identity.[5] We were created to live in shalom—with relational peace and integrity—and to advance God's shalom everywhere in everything.

The invitation to partner in God's work existed long before sin. It's what we were created to do. And that's how it was *intended* to be.

But because Adam and Eve failed to live as God created them to live, they were removed from the garden, and everything changed. God didn't take away their role of image bearing, but their new calling and priority changed. By God's grace, they were now called to act with God to *restore* shalom and wholeness to all of creation. What if our idea of mission, service, and cross-cultural ministry weren't simply relegated to the "missionaries" or to an occasional service project or trip but became as natural to all of us as breathing? This is how we were created to live.

ISRAEL (GENESIS 12)

By the time we arrive at Genesis 12, so much has happened to deface the beautiful, picture-perfect world of Eden. Deception, murder, drunkenness, and a catastrophic flood have all invaded the story line, revealing the tragedy of human rebellion. In the midst of all this, we encounter an old, childless couple—Abraham and Sarah. God made a promise to give Abraham and Sarah a son, but it wasn't just a promise for them. God's promise to Abraham would lead to the birth of the people of Israel, the chosen descendants of Abraham. Why did God create Israel and make them the chosen nation? Sometimes our debates about all this miss the key point of the story: Abraham and his descendants (Israel) were blessed *so that they might be a blessing to the world*. The priestly, representative role of Adam and Eve was reaffirmed, and a priestly nation was promised that would represent God to the other nations.

Israel was intended to be a special nation that would give the other (Gentile) nations a picture of what God was like. The Israelites would show this through the collective life of a shalom-filled nation living under the perfect and just law of God. As they obeyed God, they would be a blessing to the surrounding nations, and other nations would encounter and come to know the true God in a personal way. Isaiah the prophet challenged his fellow Jews to be a vineyard to which the Gentiles would be drawn so they might know the "I AM." Once again, God's people are invited to be God's divine representatives to the world. And just as Adam and Eve failed at the beginning, Israel fails to fulfill its God-given calling. But the story isn't over! God's redemptive plan continues; however, the particular call of the priestly role is further clarified and defined.

AARON AND SONS (EXODUS 28)

The priestly role God originally gave to all of humanity, represented by Adam and Eve, is now entrusted to the Levites—a specific tribe of Israel. Notice how the priestly scope entrusted to God's people is getting progressively smaller (see figure on p. 34). Adam and Eve were invited to represent God within all of creation. The invitation to Aaron and his sons was to be priests for the nation of Israel. The Levitical priests were called and set apart by God to offer sacrifices on behalf of the rest of the Israelites.

How successful were Aaron and his sons in fulfilling their priestly role? They too failed to live up to their God-given position. Soon after being chosen as priests, Aaron's sons, Nadab and Abihu, decided it would be cool to experiment with the fire in their censers. God was not amused and took away their priestly role and their lives! Unfortunately, even the priestly tribe of God's chosen nation failed to effectively live out the invitation to act on God's behalf in the world. In fact, the farther we walk through the Old Testament, the more we find a growing sense of hopelessness and despair. Why in the world does God keep entrusting this significant work to people when they continue to fail and fall short?

JESUS (THE GOSPELS)

At last, Jesus enters the story, and we get a picture-perfect view of how God intended Adam to live. Jesus, the final Adam, is the perfect priest and the perfect sacrifice. Through him, we see God's radiant glory lived out up close and represented in a human life. Jesus had to deal with hypocrites, earn a living, attend to his family, and each day he faced the whole monotony of everyday life. Through him, we learn how God acts in response to adulterous women (and men?!), conniving leaders, and oppressed children. We get to see how the second Adam dealt with the brokenness of his world. Jesus lived in a world where Rome was in control, poor people were exploited, and religion often seemed to make life worse, not better, for the average person. From as early as his temptation in the desert (John 4:34) to just hours before the cross (Matt. 26:39), Jesus gives us a picture of a human life fully oriented toward God's purposes. He was completely in tune with the individual needs of anyone who crossed his path, yet he also ruled over nature, stilling storms, walking on water, and miraculously catching fish.[6] Jesus understood who he was (his identity) and why he was here (his mission).

Where the first Adam failed, the last Adam was entirely successful. With Jesus' final declaration, "It is finished" (John 19:30), the curse of evil was struck powerless, and everything changed. Just as the first Adam's disobedience perverted all of creation, the work of Christ made everything new again. His resurrection from the dead three days later removed any doubt that the world had changed, and a new chapter of the story had begun.

Just before ascending to heaven, Jesus gave these parting words, often found on missions banners in churches around the world: "Go into the world and make disciples of all nations!" (Matt. 28:19–20, my paraphrase). Missions leaders have gotten plenty of mileage out of that text, and rightfully so! It's an exclamation point on God's original invitation to join Christ's work of re-creating the world and restoring what was lost in the fall. But if we simply read these verses without considering the larger context of God's created purposes, just think how much we miss!

God's invitation to join Christ's work in the world begins to expand once again (see figure on p. 34). Jesus' earthly mission was focused in a particular time and place with his fellow Jews, but the commission he gave to his followers transcends the first-century world of Palestine. As followers of Christ, we act on his behalf wherever we are, in whatever we do. What does it look like for you and me to be the presence of Jesus where we live, work, and study today?

THE CHURCH (THE BOOK OF ACTS TO TODAY)

Within weeks of Jesus' ascension, some of the disciples who heard his parting words came together and established the church. This is *our* part of the story. Peter calls us priests (1 Peter 2:9), a great reminder that as followers of Christ we continue to live out the priestly role entrusted to us. We fulfill our priestly role by calling people to follow Jesus wherever we live and whatever we do.[7] There are two important considerations as we engage in this work: joining with Christians everywhere to *be* Christ's presence today and weaving this identity into everything we *do*.

With Christians Everywhere

Paul describes the church as the body of Christ to demonstrate our interdependence as Christians in the fulfillment of our priestly work. Paul teaches us that Christ continues to live on the earth today through his body—the church.[8] In other words, we join with followers of Jesus everywhere to live out our priestly role. So if people ask, "How does God feel about refugees, human trafficking, or the HIV/AIDS crisis?" we should be able to say, *"Look at the church!"* For those who wonder, "What does God think about the economy?" we should again be able to respond, *"Look at the church!"* You may be thinking, *I'd never tell people to look at the church to see how God feels about something.* I get that. There have been occasions throughout history when Christians have been among some of the worst offenders of all time for wielding its power to exploit the oppressed. Many of us have been deeply wounded by the church or by individual Christians. But despite these failures, the church is still the way Jesus brings about real, physical hope and salvation to the world. Even with all its foibles and problems, the church—both as an institution and through its members—has continued to make Jesus known to the world for a couple thousand years. Through the church, the hope of Jesus has traversed time zones, historical eras, and cultural revolutions to reach you and me through other faithful followers of Jesus. And now it's our turn. As we go about our lives as Christians, people should be encountering God and experiencing Christ's healing presence in our words and actions.[9]

Scattered throughout every nation around the world are ordinary Christians, simply living out the way of Jesus as they go about their daily lives. If you're part of the church of Jesus Christ, you're part of a worldwide movement that can never be stopped. Heaven is crashing into earth every minute. As each Christian takes seriously what it means to be entrusted with this opportunity and joins God in making the world a better place, suddenly a divine route opens for addressing the tragedies of our day.

No one individual, group, gender, culture, or local church can alone *fully* represent the presence of Jesus. The world can't get an accurate picture of Jesus just through my life or the collective life of my local church. Richard Mouw, president of Fuller Seminary, writes, "The image of God is parceled out among the peoples of the earth.... By looking at different individuals and groups, we get glimpses of different aspects of the full image of God."[10] You and I, together with the rest of God's people, are the visible presence of Jesus in the world today.

In Everything

To live out *our* part of this story as the church means weaving our priestly identity into every part of our lives. Politics are not somehow off-limits for Christians, but they need to be reformed. The domains of art, business, and science should be claimed for Christ, not segregated as secular distractions from the "real" work of ministry. My dad used to proudly declare, "Both my sons are in full-time ministry," and almost as an afterthought he would add, "and my daughter is a nurse." I realize that "full-time ministry" is sometimes a shorthand way of referring to people who earn their paycheck from full-time employment in a church or ministry. But what could more closely resemble full-time ministry than the work my sister does daily as a nurse, caring for cancer patients and their family members? We have to reject the notion that it's the really spiritual people who should become the pastors and missionaries. We are *all* invited to partner with God—as nurses and truck drivers, aunts and uncles, engineers and musicians, and, yes, pastors and missionaries. The problem *isn't* that the Christian community lacks doctors, farmers, businesspeople, or musicians in our midst. *The problem is that there are so few doctors, farmers, businesspeople, and musicians who are truly living out their priestly identity in their profession.* That's the central idea of this book. Most of us don't integrate our Christian identity into our daily tasks. While serving as a missionary overseas is one way of fulfilling our priestly calling, so also is serving in a local hospital near home.[11] What matters most is *how* you live out your unique vocation as a follower of Jesus Christ.

Global mission is something we *all* get to be involved in. It might involve uprooting yourself and traveling overseas, but just as likely it might mean making subtle changes in the way you go about your work and life, all without ever pulling out your passport. We all get to be part of this. This is who we were *created* to be.

EVERY NATION: BACK TO THE FUTURE! (REVELATION 21 – 22)

So where is all this headed? The story isn't over yet, but we have read the end of the book! The Scriptures culminate with John's apocalyptic vision: "Then I saw 'a new heaven and a new earth.' . . . And I heard a loud voice from the throne saying, "Look! God's dwelling place is now among the people, and he will dwell with them. They will be his people, and God himself will be with them and be their God. *'He will wipe every tear from their eyes. There will be no more death' or mourning or crying or pain*, for the old order of things has passed away" (Rev. 21:1, 3–4, emphasis added).

Everlasting worship. Authentic relationships. Pure water. Flawless beauty. Worshipers from every nation. It's going to happen. When we live as we were intended to live, we become part of a whole new world that is bursting forth. We don't engage in mission because somehow if we don't, Jesus is going to slip off the throne. The outcome is clear: Jesus *will* be worshiped by "every nation, tribe, people and language" (Rev. 7:9). The broken order of things will pass away. Harmony in our relationships, oneness with God, and shalom will once again characterize everything.

Our lives ought to be fully shaped by this future reality. Our work today is not in vain. In due time, it *will* become part of God's new world. The New Testament scholar N. T. Wright says it well: "Every act of love, gratitude, and kindness; every work of art or music inspired by the love of God and delight in the beauty of his creation; every minute spent teaching a severely handicapped child to read or walk; every act of care and nurture, of support and comfort, for one's fellow human beings and for that matter one's fellow non-human creatures; and of course every prayer, all Spirit-led teaching, every deed that spreads the gospel, builds up the church, embraces and embodies holiness rather than corruption, and makes the name of Jesus honored in the world — *all of this will find its way, through the resurrecting power of God, into the new creation that God will one day make.*"[12]

I don't fully grasp how my actions today will find their way into my life in eternity. But I do know I can go about my work today with an assurance that it's connected to the whole new world God is making. I don't plan to strum a harp on a cloud for all of eternity. We're headed back toward Eden-like perfection and harmony, but the future city described for us in Revelation will be very different from the undeveloped, prehistoric garden in Genesis 1. The entire universe is moving from a garden to a city.[13] Medical, technological, and architectural developments are all expressions of countless generations living out their role as cocreators with God, and we can expect vestiges of these developments to be with us forever. Abundant evils taint urbanization, many of our technological advances, the art of filmmaking, and our contemporary scientific research, yet the advancement of these developments are also a part of the world God is bringing forth.[14] The story ends where it began, with our living as we were created to live — in a perfect, harmonious universe, where we will reign with God as cocreators for ever and ever (Rev. 22:5).

This is who we are.

This is why we're here.

GOD'S INVITATION TO YOU

The competition against living as we were created to live is immense. Everyone seems to want a piece of our imagination. We're bombarded with messages that try to socialize us for something other than our true identity as partners with God. The subtext goes something like this: *Imagine being the envy of everyone at the gym because of how hard you've been working out. Picture yourself at the top of your game by outselling everyone on your team. Save enough today, and someday you can have the retirement of your dreams. Buy this product, and you will have a whole new sex appeal.* On and on, these attempts try to convince us that we were made for more money, more success, more sex, and more independence. But these promises all fall short: you were made for so much more! Each of us contains the divine spark of God and was created to be a partner in moving creation forward to the consummation of God's purposes.

God chose to be limited by working through us. God "cannot" do some things unless we *work*. When a new bridge, database software, or literacy program is needed, will God just miraculously cause it to drop from heaven? "That is an absurd and idle fatalism. God stores the hills with marble, but never built a Parthenon; God fills the mountains with ore, but never made a needle or locomotive."[15] God has decided that it's only when we work that some things will be done—whether our work is caring for our kids or aging parents, building homes, starting a business, or farming.

We are invited to join God in redeeming this world. When we feel a compulsion to do something in response to tragic circumstances, we're tapping into something deeply connected to how we were created to live. If God calls you to move overseas to respond to the aches and groans of our world, go for it. But this book is mainly for the rest of us, who are trying to make a difference from our own backyards.

BEFORE YOU TURN THE PAGE

Put yourself in the story. Draw yourself (stick figures are fine!) where you fit into God's story (between "The Church" and "Every Nation"!).

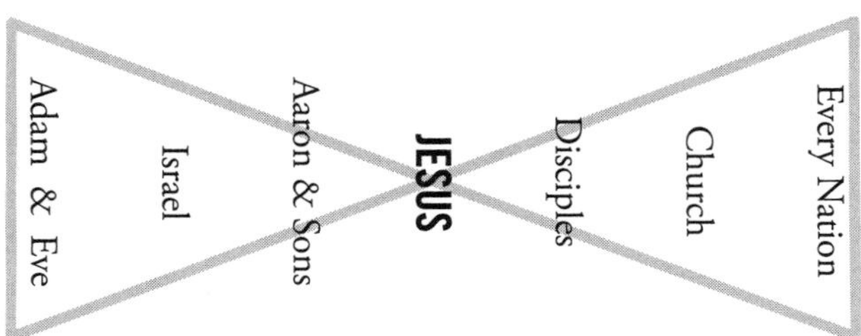

What encourages you about viewing your identity as a partner with God in the world?

What challenges you about viewing your life this way?

What do you need to explore further?

CHAPTER 3

SPEAK UP NOW

SEVEN STRATEGIES YOU CAN USE TODAY

Seeing the challenges faced by our global neighbors (chapter 1) puts things in perspective for us, and the invitation to partner with God (chapter 2) is an inspiration. But the fact remains: one billion people will still go to bed hungry tonight. Every minute, another person is being trafficked into the sex industry and other forced labor; and one-third of our global population has tuberculosis. How do we ensure that the statistics in chapter 1 and the ideas we looked at in chapter 2 actually make the world a better place?

I'm easily motivated by rock-star-like individuals who instigate sweeping reforms that garner a great deal of public attention. People like Mother Teresa, Nelson Mandela, Rick Warren, Bill and Melinda Gates, and Bono inspire me. But I'm even *more* excited by grassroots revolutionaries who make a difference without ever being noticed. These are people who aren't trying to change the world all by themselves. But neither can they simply turn a blind eye and go on with life as usual when confronted with injustice and evil.

I was recently reading the Old Testament story of Naaman, the Syrian general whose world came crashing down when he got leprosy (2 Kings 5). Pre-leprosy, Naaman had the ear of the king and was living the high life. I imagine him hanging out on the equivalent of royal golf courses and being escorted by an entourage of servants wherever he went. He was in control of everything and everyone in his life. But then he was plagued with leprosy. Leprosy quickly turns even the most noble and powerful into social outcasts. Once word got out that he was a leper, he would quickly be uninvited from all the royal functions. And any media attention he received would be negative.

Visualize Naaman and his wife preparing for one more elaborate party, just before the public learns about his diagnosis. Perhaps "Mrs. Naaman" is in her private quarters primping for the banquet, with the realization that life as they've known it is about to end. Assisting the general's wife is a young, respectful servant woman. Servants are the underdogs, but they are the ones who get an honest glimpse into the personal world of royalty. This servant girl knows what the public doesn't—General Naaman has leprosy. She's a lowly slave, but she cares about the general and his wife.

The only record of this woman's existence are these brief words: "If only my master would see the prophet [Elisha] who is in Samaria! He would cure him of his leprosy" (2 Kings 5:3). That's it! That's all we hear from her. But the entire story of Naaman's life changes because this God-fearing servant girl speaks up. Old Testament scholar Walter Brueggemann notes four things about this servant girl:

1. She attended to the need right in front of her.
2. She remembered her true identity and knew God could work through Elisha and her.
3. She spoke hope into sadness.
4. She opened up a new realm of possibility to the otherwise hopeless.[1]

This young girl was ready to act on God's behalf, and she spoke up. She wasn't paralyzed or discouraged by her lowly job. She took the opportunities she was given and had a larger view of what God could do (and did!) through her faithfulness.

I'm afraid I would have missed this opportunity. I often spend more time focusing on the future than on the present. In high school I couldn't wait to get to college. Then, in college I was pining to get out into the real world and make a difference, instead of just reading textbooks. The early days of my career were spent thinking about how much more I could do *someday* in a *better* job. I find that I'm often so obsessed with making a difference in the future that I easily miss opportunities staring me right in the face today.

Most of the remainder of this book is devoted to helping us think long-term about making a difference in the world through our varied jobs and interests. But before we go there, I want to suggest seven strategies each of us can begin practicing right now to speak up on behalf of our global neighbors.

1. BE AWARE

The first step is developing global awareness. Statistics by themselves don't make life better for anyone, but a basic understanding of what life is like for our neighbors near and far is essential. I don't expect that everyone has the time to keep up with all the latest figures on poverty and disease. But we should never forget that the numbers and issues represent real lives and circumstances.

We North Americans, in particular, continue to fair poorly when tested for our global consciousness. Recent research among U.S. adults shows:

- Only one in seven can find Iraq on a world map.[2]
- Only 8 percent can name the prime minister of Canada.[3]
- 72 percent believe that all devout Muslims support killing non-Muslims (though the majority of Muslims around the world refute this statement).[4]
- Only one in five has a passport.[5]

You have to search beyond the mainstream news to get much of an understanding of what's going on globally. Events in developing countries make headlines only when another atrocity erupts or a disaster occurs. It's especially rare to hear *good* news about people and events in Africa. Where are the stories about the growing move away from dictatorships to democracy, the efforts of African institutions to combat disease and ecological degradation, and the commitment of many African governments to alleviate poverty? By ignoring

Seven Strategies

1. Be aware
2. Inform and recruit others
3. Work it into work
4. Give
5. Shop responsibly
6. Invest/divest
7. Influence government and media

the positive news, much of the Western media sends the message that the entire continent is hopeless. Similar stories go unreported from other developing parts of the world.[6]

A few ways to enhance your global consciousness include:

- Visit BBC news (*http://news.bbc.co.uk/*) for one of the more robust purviews of world events.
- Check out *www.worldpress.org* for a quick overview of current stories globally.
- Visit *www.languagemonitor.com* to see the top ten words of the year.
- Tune into public broadcasting.
- Consume a variety of news sources to see how the "same" events get reported differently.

Increased global awareness is one of the great benefits of international travel, if the travel is done well. When we travel abroad and see firsthand what's happening, CNN, Fox News, and missionary updates are no longer our sole informants. Be careful not to rush to judgment based on a brief encounter abroad, but use travel to enhance your awareness about life for our global neighbors. Opening our eyes to the needs around us is the first step toward action.

2. INFORM AND RECRUIT OTHERS

As you learn about various issues, weave them into your conversations. Don't be the obnoxious global-chip-on-your-shoulder person who puts people on guilt trips at every turn. Instead look for ways to interject stories about our global neighbors. When selling or buying a coffee blend from Ethiopia, reference how inspiring it is to see East Africans' resourcefulness despite ongoing war and poverty in the region. When caring for a group of kids who say, "We're hungry," gently describe what hunger means for many kids around the world. As you have lunch with a friend, talk about an underreported news story. When you're at a family gathering, speak up when a racist joke is told. Use a writing or speech assignment to learn about an issue and inform others in your class.

The organizationally savvy may want to go further by coordinating a walkathon to raise money and awareness for a particular cause. Or you might develop an online network to coordinate efforts to grow awareness, prayer, advocacy, and funding. Perhaps you could start a local organization that convenes around a concern or join other organizations already doing something like this. Check out *www.enoughproject.org* for an example of an organized effort to grow awareness and response to genocide and mass atrocities.

Don't underestimate the role of informing others. Amy Butler, a pastor at Calvary Baptist Church in Washington, D.C., made a commitment to mention the Sudanese crisis at every Sunday worship service for an entire season. She never had to suggest starting a church program for Sudan. The congregation naturally responded to their increased awareness, and a grassroots initiative began as a result.

What happens when there's a horrible crisis that requires global intervention, and not enough citizens make a noise about it? Nothing.[7] People can't be expected to care about something they don't know about. Recruiting others to join you in your service begins with increasing their awareness.

3. WORK IT INTO WORK

Most of us can speak up through our work, something we'll address more fully in part 2 of the book. But what about those who work at a blue-collar job? Our global village can't function if everyone sits behind a desk or wears a lab coat. Society is dependent on those who are willing to work long hours digging ditches, plumbing, installing heating units, and working along assembly lines.

Some people working in manufacturing jobs might find little satisfaction in their work because they have a hard time seeing how the widget they produce fulfills their priestly calling. Maybe you work all day making some small part of an electronic device, and you wonder if what you do really meets a pressing need in the world. There *can* be redemptive value even in jobs like yours: doing your work with excellence, contributing to the larger provision of goods and services, praying for the people who will use the products, and recommending and implementing safety practices to improve the lives of fellow workers are just a few examples. There are people at your workplace whom you can love and encourage, and even more, your family receives the loving benefit of the income you earn from your employment.

Employees *can* influence their workplace to be an agent for God's work in the world. For example, my friend Adam works as a computer programmer for a large grocery store company. Most days he sits in a cubicle working on various projects for the company. He has observed the increased attention his company is giving to marketing and selling organic products. Since he is concerned about the environment and health issues, he celebrates this initiative. But he'd like to see the same kind of spotlight put on selling "slave-free" products. He's approaching management with some ideas about how they can be on the competitive edge of selling a line of products like this while also doing good in the world.

Whenever possible as you search for a job, look for an employer that practices corporate social responsibility. Find out about their international labor practices and their commitment to environmental responsibility. Ask whether they have a foundation through which they'll match employee contributions to charities.

There are countless other ways Christians can live out Christ's presence in the world through the work they do. There are lawyers doing pro bono defense work for those unable to afford it, politicians working for legislation that brings about redemptive change in cities and nations, and pilots safely transporting people from one side of the world to the other. There are third-shift factory workers who make parts of gadgets that make our lives safer, and while they work, they relate graciously with their immigrant coworkers. There are retail associates dealing with cantankerous customers in ways that embody the grace of Jesus, and baristas who serve people with a smile and use their coffee shop as a platform for advocacy. Construction workers are taking into account how they care for the environment and fixing the homes of people in need. Military personnel, police officers, and firefighters are protecting us, farmers are feeding us, and truck drivers are getting goods to people near and far. Meanwhile many stay-at-home parents are working for love, sometimes *only* for love.[8] Look around you for creative ways to connect your global concerns with your work!

4. GIVE

Donating money is the most common response we're offered when confronted with global needs. But giving money to a cause doesn't have to be something you do just on your own. Recruit your friends and family members to join you in raising money for a cause. Garage sales, benefit concerts, party fund-raisers, and walkathons are just a few of the many fund-raising strategies that your group can use. You won't have to look far for ideas and for initiatives you can join.

You can't fund everything, but you can get involved somewhere with the people and causes dear to your heart. Do a little homework to be sure your gifts actually reach the poor and oppressed. Look for groups that cut unnecessary spending and operational costs in order for your money to have the greatest possible impact.

Most of us feel the enormity of our own financial pressures. But don't wait until you strike it rich to start giving and sharing. Start where you are and give a little. Then find ways to gradually increase what you can give.

5. SHOP RESPONSIBLY

The sugar boycott in the late 1700s was one of the earliest examples of consumers using their purchasing power to bring about change. During that time, sugar was primarily produced on the backs of slaves. An enraged public boycotted sugar, and sales dropped by half! Some shops advertised goods that weren't produced by slaves and saw their sales increase tenfold over two years.[9] Similar efforts are occurring today through the fair trade movement and through groups like Stop the Traffik (*www.stopthetraffik.org*).

Take some time to learn more about the products you buy, especially those you purchase most regularly and the ones that cost you the most money. Ask things like:

- Where and how was this produced?
- What raw materials were used in its production?
- What impact did producing this have on the environment? (Visit *www.biggreenpurse.com.*)
- What sort of ethical track record is behind the companies involved?[10]

Visit *www.shoppingforabetterworld.com* for additional ideas and for help on wielding our power as consumers to extend God's reach.

6. INVEST/DIVEST

Examine the companies you invest in, in light of their labor practices and environmental commitments. We should see our dollars producing returns there as well. Socially responsible investing (SRI) is a growing movement that measures social and environmental practices of companies as well as financial criteria.

Assess the holdings of your investments to see if the companies involved reflect your values. Invest in "social funds," which function like normal mutual funds but institute social screens as well, barring certain types of companies (for example, cigarette manufacturers, major polluters, and so on), and seek out exceptional social performers based on their sustainability practices, community investments, no-sweat-shop policies, and other factors.[11] For help understanding the SRI movement, visit *www.socialinvest.org*.

Hold your investment companies and pension plans accountable for divesting from funds that support corrupt regimes. Growing numbers of state pensions and investment companies are divesting from funds that directly or even indirectly support malicious dictators. The Khartoum government in Sudan is being starved financially because of efforts like these. Activists are helping cut off the funding for the genocidal campaign in Darfur, particularly by divesting from many oil and energy funds.[12] Visit *www.sudandivestment.org* to see what you can do. A few phone calls and transactions can be part of living out your role as God's partner in the ways your money is used for good and not evil.

7. INFLUENCE GOVERNMENT AND MEDIA

Finally, send a letter, stop a genocide. It sounds too simplistic, doesn't it? But Senator Paul Simon said that a mere one hundred letters to each member of Congress could have changed the outcome of the genocide in Rwanda. Congresspeople often say, "We have to hear from our constituents. Make as much noise as you can, scream bloody murder, force us to care!"[13] It's easy for us to become jaded by the corruption in the political system, but remember: not every government leader is driven by selfish motives. Writing letters to Congress, having face-to-face meetings with local officials, and sending letters to the editor of your local paper *can* raise public awareness of problems like genocide and human trafficking. In their extremely helpful book *Not on Our Watch*, Hollywood actor Don Cheadle and activist John Prendergast say that they want to see more and more people "nagging" their legislators to vote on behalf of those suffering from genocide. Cheadle and Prendergast write, "We need to tell [elected officials], 'We're mad as hell and we aren't going to vote for you anymore!' "[14] Then *affirm* those politicians who do act on behalf of the oppressed.

Our treatment of the media should be similar. It's easy to get revved up about how little airtime is given to these issues. But the media, like any business, simply respond to the interests and demands of viewers. The news media need to hear from citizens in order to prioritize news and programs and focus on those we care about. There's even something to be said for applying similar pressure on religious leaders and pastors who may have the attention of large groups of church attendees.

Here's a specific word to college students who might view their influence as limited or, at best, delayed until they graduate from college. Historically, when governmental power has been threatened, it's usually the students who are feared the most. In the midst of a coup, dictators will often shut down the universities before doing anything else. Consider the revolutions that took place at the Berlin Wall, in Tiananmen Square, or during the 2009 Iranian elections to get a glimpse of the powerful ways that students can influence their governments and gain the attention of the news media. Don't view your time in school as merely biding time until you can get into the real action. Use your voice to speak up now.

GET STARTED!

An injustice like extreme poverty requires the continued apathy of others to exist. Environmental decay will keep making life worse for people around the world if we simply ignore pressing problems. Feeling paralyzed by the despair of human trafficking does nothing to help those who are being trafficked. God is making his appeal through us, and it's time for us to "speak up for those who cannot speak for themselves.... Defend the rights of the poor and needy" (Prov. 31:8–9).

There are many ways you can speak up, show up, and stand up. Whatever our circumstances right now, the overarching question we can each ask is, *How can I use my power, technology, education, job, relationships, money, family, and skills in light of the needs of the world?* All of us, as citizens, family members, and friends, can speak up on behalf of our neighbors.

Don't discount what God can do through you. Every one of us can make a global difference. In the words of the late Senator Robert Kennedy, "Let no one be discouraged by the belief there is nothing one man or woman can do against an enormous array of the world's ills—against misery and ignorance, injustice and violence.... Few will have the greatness to bend history itself; but each of us can work to change a small portion of events, and in the total of all those acts will be written the history of this generation.... It is from the numberless diverse acts of courage and belief that human history is shaped. Each time a man stands up for an ideal, or acts to improve the lots of others, or strikes out against injustice, he sends a tiny ripple of hope, and crossing each other from a million different centers of energy and daring, those ripples build a current which can sweep down the mightiest walls of oppression and resistance."[15]

Start right where you are. Respond to God's invitation and speak up for your global neighbors.

BEFORE YOU TURN THE PAGE

Review the seven strategies from this chapter:

1. Be aware
2. Inform and recruit others
3. Work it into work
4. Give
5. Shop responsibly
6. Invest/divest
7. Influence government and media

Identify one of these strategies you can use in the next week. How will you use it? What will you do? Be specific.

Identify an additional strategy you can use in the next month. How will you use it? What will you do? Again, be specific.

PART 2

A SMALL (LIMITED YET ESSENTIAL) CONTRIBUTION

It's time for us to move from a big-picture understanding of our calling and context to take a closer look at the tangible and specific contributions each of us can add — one by one — to make a world of difference. This section is filled with ideas and stories of how people are making a difference in the world through various passions, skills, relationships, and circumstances. Many of the topics and stories relate closely to a particular field of work, including owning a business, teaching, and engineering. But there's something here for each of us. Even though I don't work in the arts, I was made to create. You might not be in business, but you make businesslike decisions regularly. Some study the body and mind for decades, but all of us care about our health. And we all have friends working in these various contexts.

Of course, there's no way for me to include every profession. But even those who can't find their job in one of these chapters can learn from the examples and stories of others. I've included a few larger-than-life examples from those exceptional few who are written up in books and talked about on TV. But the vast majority of the stories in these chapters are about ordinary people like you and me who are simply trying to make a small but essential contribution to God's work in this world. The people you'll read about aren't trying to save the world all by themselves; they're partnering with God and others to do something. And they're saving themselves from the death of indifference. Together we can all extend God's reach into this world and help reverse the curse of evil that gnaws at every turn.

CHAPTER 4

WHAT'S THE REAL BOTTOM LINE?

BUSINESS AND MANAGEMENT

One by one, the MBA students walked across the stage to receive their diplomas. Admittedly, I wasn't paying much attention to anyone else at that moment. I was just hoping I wouldn't trip when my name was called. I was sitting next to one of my professors, and I suddenly heard her murmur, "Ah, yes. There go the corporate warmongers, unleashed to pillage the world with their greed." I didn't know whether to laugh, ignore her, or start an argument. I decided on a noncommittal smirk, but her offhanded comment reminds me that many academics and activists devoted to these global concerns view business leaders as the enemy of the poor and oppressed.

Ironically, I now spend a lot of time working with business executives. And while some of them fit my professor's description to a T, others defy it in every way. *What does it mean to be God's partner in the world of business?*

We're not after some pie-in-the-sky, "Don't worry about the bottom line" notion. If a business isn't profitable, it won't be a business for very long. The challenge instead is for business leaders to determine how their work can be extended beyond their personal and corporate interests. Rather than following the drive for greater power, wealth, and success, business professionals need to ask: What value-added service do we offer our customers? How are the profits of our business being used? What kinds of business practices are we engaged in? How does our business intersect with the global issues of our day?

TRIPLE BOTTOM LINE

John Elkington, dubbed the "dean of the corporate social responsibility movement," first coined the term "triple bottom line" to suggest that businesses need to be equally responsible for their fiscal profits, people, and the planet. He argued that all three of these benchmarks are key indicators of today's successful business: Are we profitable, and if so, what goes along with the *profits* being made? Are we causing *people* suffering, despair, or injustice in the process of making a profit? And how does our work affect the *planet*?[1]

Profits

It's hard to imagine a successful company that isn't profitable. Presumably, the reason a company exists is to offer a service or product to a group of customers. Without profits, it's difficult, if not impossible, to fulfill that purpose.

There are some fascinating conversations about the role of capitalism in making the world a better place. Clearly, we need to think about the boundaries and limits of profit-seeking and ask when a system like capitalism has gone too far, reducing society to nothing more than producers and consumers. But it's also appropriate to ask which problems in the world are too great to be solved by governments and charitable work alone. As companies expand their production capabilities to meet more needs of people in the developed world, new skills and incomes become available to people living in the developing world.

There's been a great deal of attention given to Bill Gates' transition from CEO of Microsoft to cochairing the Gates Foundation with his wife, Melinda. I'm thankful for the Gates' attention to global issues like education, HIV/AIDS, and poverty. But some economists suggest Gates did more to help the poor as a businessman than he ever will as a philanthropist. His multinational corporation created new jobs for people all over the world and offered a more effective way for people to do their work and manage their lives. The Microsoft Word program I'm using to write this manuscript is a result of Gates' wildly successful business. Furthermore, Gates gained the opportunity to be staggeringly generous *because* he was a profit-producing capitalist. These are certainly complex issues, and it is wise for business leaders to explore these complexities, but we must also be aware that when corporations find new markets in developing countries, they often bring about an increased opportunity for jobs. Other businesses help initiate local start-ups in developing countries through creative partnerships with manufacturers, helping them to reach a global market.[2] Starting new businesses and giving people jobs is just one way business leaders can leverage their fiscal profits for good purposes.

Even Bono has tapped into the profit-making side of business with his RED Campaign. By paying a little extra for a RED Gap T-shirt or a RED iPod, you can help fund efforts to reduce AIDS in Africa. Socially concerned consumers often choose to purchase these products because they're associated with a cause, which in turn enhances profitability for the participating companies. At least that's the rationale behind the idea. Granted, campaigns like this aren't without some potential weaknesses. For example, wouldn't we do more to prevent AIDS by giving directly to the cause than by doing so through the Gap? But the objective is for business leaders to consider responsible and creative ways of making profits while supporting redemptive goals.

People

The second bottom line is people. This is the degree to which a business enhances the quality of life for people through the product or service they offer. And it's the way employees, vendors, outsourced labor, customers, and humanity at large are affected by a company's practices.

Employees

Some of our dearest friends, Jon and Ginger Goad, were one of the earliest examples Linda and I saw of business owners who placed an unusually high value on people by the way they treated their employees. Jon and Ginger's packaging business required a slew of manual laborers to work in their factory. The Goads wanted to find a way to offer jobs to people who were typically passed over because of physical and mental disabilities or as a result of not being able to drive to a job. So they arranged to have a van bring employees back and forth to work every day. In addition, the annual Christmas party wasn't just for the head honcho suit-types. Everyone in the company was invited. Christmas parties were a wild array of ethnic and class diversity.

One way to raise the people bottom line is to protest discrimination and hire competent individuals from marginalized subcultures. What demographics are represented among personnel? Is there an intentional effort to offer jobs to individuals who might not otherwise get one, or does management hire people just like themselves? Or consider the wages paid. Are employees merely compensated what a business can get away with paying them, or is there a spirit of sharing profits with everyone involved in the company's success?

Think creatively about how to care for employees. Single parents often need more flexibility and options for day care. College students hired for minimum wage are often in need of new work experiences and tuition assistance. Older staff members might have different needs than middle-aged personnel. Expectant and new parents have unique concerns. And sensitivity to various religious faiths can go a long way in demonstrating respect and care. Christian business leaders should be exemplary employers.

Vendors and Outsourced Labor

Attending to the people bottom line also refers to the practices and conditions of other businesses and laborers involved in a company's success. A clothing manufacturer that says they don't hire children or have sweatshop conditions in their factories is great, but what about the factories to which they subcontract work? Who regulates whether a Malaysian factory providing outsourced labor is treating its people in a humanizing way? Being Christ's presence in business includes conducting due diligence to learn whether ethical and respectful labor practices are used by the subcontractors you hire.

Cadbury, one of the world's largest chocolate distributors, responded to customers who were outraged by chocolate slaves. Earlier I shared that more than 35 percent of the world's chocolate is made from cocoa beans grown in Côte d'Ivoire, a country where children are forced to work all day long. A similar travesty occurs in nearby Ghana, where Cadbury established cocoa farms more than a hundred years ago. Cadbury has committed to partner with the Fairtrade Federation to stop using slave-harvested cocoa for producing chocolate. Todd Stitzer, CEO at Cadbury, said, "I was in Ghana and saw how vital it is that businesses support their partners and the communities they live in.... Last year we launched the Cadbury Cocoa Partnership—after all, what's good for the farmers is good for our customers and our business."[3]

Customers

Customers are another part of the people measurement in determining the bottom-line profit. To what degree is your pricing attainable and appropriate? Tiered pricing may sometimes be needed to make products available to those who otherwise would be unable to afford them. Some corporations are allowing their top innovators to spend part of their time working on creative solutions to issues facing people who are too poor to be customers. For example, Microsoft has unleashed some of its very best minds in its research lab in India to work on new products, technologies, and business models that make computing more accessible and affordable. Bill Gates said, "In one case, we're developing an interface that will enable illiterate or semi-literate people to use a PC instantly, with minimal training or assistance. In another we're looking at how wireless, together with software, can ... [enhance] access in rural areas."[4] Business leaders can enlist staff who find common ground between the interests of the company and the interests of the poor.

Corporate executives and boards should be asking, Is the product or service our business offers enhancing the life of our customers? Is there ever a time we'd give up a profit-producing opportunity because the liabilities for people outweigh the benefits?

Planet

The third bottom line is caring for the environment. Almost every business has jumped on this bandwagon now, but this is a good trend! If you're not already recycling products in your office or workplace, develop a plan to do so. Find people in your organization who are passionate about this cause and empower them to implement a recycling program. Encourage your employees to brainstorm creative strategies that can help make you a more green company. How can you reduce packaging? Is your current packaging recyclable? How can you educate and enable your consumers to recycle more?

Ocean Minded, a California-based shoe company, is very intentional about their environmental bottom line. They believe that oceans and beaches are our most natural playgrounds, so they use only recycled and sustainable materials in making their shoes. They organize beach and waterway cleanups around the world, and they educate customers about the importance of keeping oceans and beaches pollution free. Although making and selling shoes is their primary focus, Ocean Minded is also helping save the fish in our oceans and waterways, which in turn helps billions of people who rely on seafood for daily nourishment.

Going green can often save businesses money. Companies as large as Wal-Mart have discovered this. After listening to their consumers, Wal-Mart acknowledged the vast amount of planet damage being done by their expanding business. It took the devastation of Hurricane Katrina to really open the eyes of Wal-Mart's CEO, Lee Scott. When Scott saw the positive role Wal-Mart played in utilizing their people and resources to deal with the devastation of Katrina, he became convinced Wal-Mart could also use their size and resources to make the earth a better place for all of us. As a result, Wal-Mart set goals to increase the fuel efficiency of their fleet of trucks, saving them millions of dollars per year while at the same time reducing pollution. They also reduced energy use in their stores through more efficient lighting, heating, and cooling, and they began making energy-saving products like compact fluorescent lightbulbs (CFLs) more affordable for customers. A new packaging strategy was launched, minimizing the amount of packaging used and the waste produced. These changes have meant saving space—and costs for the company—while also demonstrating wise stewardship of our environment.[5]

Tim Sanders, author of *Saving the World at Work*, says, "If 100 million Wal-Mart customers replaced just one traditional light bulb with a CFL, the daily energy savings could provide a day's worth of electricity for a city of 1.5 million people."[6] Of course, many question Wal-Mart's motives and whether the company is really committed to the environment or simply committed to finding new ways of raising their profits. But that's the point: *the two aren't mutually exclusive.* Even behemoths like Wal-Mart have found creative ways to *simultaneously* reduce their carbon footprint and save money.

Businesses of all sizes and types can commit to strategies that engage the triple bottom line. David and Danielle Bult moved from the United States to Morocco to start Green Sahara, a small furniture company. They use only sustainably harvested wood, pay their employees (Moroccans) a decent wage, and work fairly with local artisans (also Moroccans). They want to make the world a better place for people to work and live. Green Sahara is committed to helping Moroccans benefit from their natural resources without killing off those resources in the process.

As you can see, financial responsibility doesn't *necessarily* conflict with a commitment to greater humanitarian and environmental care. There may be times when we give up a profit-producing opportunity because it violates the other two bottom lines. But the emphasis here is more on how we operate and use finances. Money can be used to offer people opportunities, sustenance, and empowerment—or it can be used to destroy life.[7]

START YOUR OWN BUSINESS

One way to extend Christ's reach as a businessperson is to start a company like Green Sahara and Ocean Minded Shoes—businesses oriented around social and environmental missions as well as financial ones. The innovative skills and risk tolerance of entrepreneurs are some of the most valuable tools available for responding to global causes. Start-ups like these may look like any other business on the outside, but they're guided by Christ-centered values from within. Other entrepreneurs may break with traditional models and develop companies or products specifically oriented toward a particular cause or need in the world.

Fleetwood Group is a business that is committed to being a Christ-centered electronics and furniture company. The products they sell and many of the business models they use are very similar to those used by their competitors. But the founders started the business with a different orientation and a different purpose. They financially support cross-cultural ministry projects and connect interested employees to missionaries through a prayer partnership program. They also give employees paid time off to participate in various service projects.

An even more innovative model can be seen through a fair trade T-shirt company started by an American couple with Ivy League business degrees. They were deeply disturbed by the conflict between Israel and Palestine, so they visited the region to see what was happening firsthand. They built relationships with the Palestinian people who lived there, and began to see a huge need for jobs. As a result, they began a T-shirt company that now employs nearly a hundred Palestinians.[8]

Another example of innovation that incorporates humanitarian concern is Cred, a jewelry company that emerged from a group of British jewelers who were incensed by the blood diamond market. They traveled to Bolivia, Columbia, and across Africa finding people who worked in the diamond industry. They built personal relationships with them and developed a business plan using this motto: "From the moment [the diamond] was mined till it goes on your finger, every worker was treated with dignity and respect."[9] Is this a creative marketing strategy? Possibly, but it's redemptive nonetheless!

These are just a few examples of what is looks like when do-it-yourself entrepreneurs engage the triple bottom line. They combine their business innovation or an ability to make profits, with a love for people and the planet. If you have an entrepreneurial streak, consider how you can use it to serve your global neighbors through a new business.

WORKING FOR THE MACHINE

While some individuals are called to start entrepreneurial ventures, many business leaders are better suited to live out their priestly role within someone else's company. Even if the company you work for isn't guided by things like the triple bottom line, don't underestimate what you can do by simply living out the words and actions of Jesus in your workplace.

Clive Mather, a former Shell executive, believes that his life as a business leader can't be compartmentalized from his life as a Christian. In a compelling essay on globalization, Mather writes, "I am writing not only from my perspective as Chairman of Shell UK, but also as a parent, a Christian, and a member of the global community. These roles are closely intertwined. Even if I wanted to write solely as a business leader, it would be impossible."[10]

Mather was a major leader in developing Shell's guiding ethics against child labor. Today the youngest Shell employee in the world is sixteen years old and lives in the United States. These aren't simple issues to regulate. For example, energy companies in Brazil have historically been required by law to add 15 percent ethanol from local sugar cane production to their fuel. In Brazil, the majority of sugar cane is harvested by children. Shell, with the leadership of Mather, went directly to the Brazilian government and became an advocate to end child labor. Soon afterward, Shell introduced a clause in its contracts with distillers forbidding the use of child labor and asking them to respect Shell's position or find another business partner. In addition, Shell helped set up funds to provide an education for these children, who would otherwise have no option but to go find work elsewhere to help their families.[11]

Companies as large as Shell are certainly not immune from making mistakes when it comes to pressing human rights issues and the environment. But within these companies are Christians like Mather who have chosen to respond to the issues of poverty, injustice, and trafficking *through their business careers*. Even businesspeople who don't have executive roles can do their part. Treating colleagues and customers with respect, advocating for humanitarian practices, starting a recycling campaign in your unit, and organizing a department-wide fund-raiser for a cause are just a few ways ordinary business employees are speaking up in companies around the world. And above all, doing our work with excellence and seeing our tasks as something that can contribute to God's increased reign in the world are key motivations for all of us. Take some time to look carefully at your work in the business world and contemplate how you might be an agent of change from within.

PAY IT FORWARD

Another growing movement among many businesses is *philanthropically supporting* local and global endeavors. Granted, business philanthropy sometimes seems to be as much about marketing as anything else. But the mixed motives of some business leaders shouldn't keep us from looking at how business leaders can give back to their communities in big and small ways. You don't need to be a C-level executive in a Fortune 500 company to do this. An employee of a small construction company can volunteer with other employees one evening a month to fix the homes of the elderly or to do an "extreme makeover" for a local family in need. Hairstylists can give free haircuts to the jobless, to the homeless, or to those with chronic illnesses. Restaurant owners can take a cue from several Washington, D.C., restaurants that recently asked their customers to pay one dollar for a glass of tap water and in turn gave 100 percent of the proceeds to communities without clean drinking water.[12]

Some organizations give their employees one week of paid time to do volunteer service somewhere in the world. This allows the organization to contribute to something bigger than itself. In return, employees tap into one of the greatest tools for their development and training in a global marketplace—international travel.[13] One Los Angeles–based manufacturing company has created a foundation wherein the company helps provide clean water filters for several communities throughout Sub-Saharan Africa. They offer employees one week of paid time to do volunteer service in one of these regions. Employees can even apply for grant money from the company's foundation to help fund their trips.[14]

I recently spent time with some executives from Timberland, a well-known company with a reputation for "paying it forward." In December 2006, Timberland held a conference for its sales reps in New Orleans, fifteen months after Hurricane Katrina. On the first night of the conference, local leaders were invited to talk to the sales reps about the struggle to rebuild New Orleans. On the second day, two hundred sales reps were taken by bus to the Central City district to work on a neighborhood restoration project. In just a few hours, the Timberland employees, working alongside local volunteers, had a prominent restaurant ready for reopening. Before the sales reps returned to their conference, the meeting organizers gave them a tour of the Ninth Ward, one of the city's most devastated areas. The sales reps were sobered by how much work still had to be done to rebuild the city.

As the reps walked through some of these ravaged neighborhoods, one of them got into a conversation with a local resident, who said, "Shoes, used ones, new ones—we need shoes." Many of the neighborhood residents were running around barefoot or wearing flip-flops, and there were rusty nails and splintered boards everywhere. The Timberland employee unlaced his boots on the spot and handed them to the resident. Another coworker did the same. In the next ten minutes, the buses emptied out as all two hundred sales reps walked over to the community center and donated their shoes to the Ninth Ward.[15]

Over the next several months, Timberland employees became even more involved in the struggle to rebuild New Orleans. All of this began with a senior leader who valued community service as part of the company's sales conference. And all it took was one sales rep to respond to a need that he could meet right then. Don't underestimate what you can accomplish when you too have an opportunity to pay it forward. Just start with the needs right in front of you.

DOING GODLY BUSINESS

Writing checks to missionaries, praying, and going on short-term missions trips are all valid ways for businesspeople to partner with God. But there are many other strategic opportunities we should consider. Our invitation to join God's work includes dealing with things like safety standards, child labor practices, and discrimination in hiring. Practicing environmental responsibility, producing and delivering products and services that address the pressing needs of our world, and simply improving the quality of life for people are all ways we embody the presence of Jesus as a businessperson.

Nancy Koehn, a Harvard business professor, writes, "Business is the most powerful force for change on the global stage right now. No other set of institutions — not religious organizations, not the nation-state, not individual NGOs — has the resources or breadth and on-the-ground depth of business to deal with what is in front of us today. Yes, all these other players matter, in some cases a great deal. But not as much as business — in the form of both large, global corporations and small-scale entrepreneurial enterprises."[16]

We can debate whether Koehn is right about the preeminent power of business to enact change, but the point remains: business leaders can engage in wide-scale redemptive activity that touches people globally.

Imagine business professionals engaged in transforming and building the economic and business culture of our world in ways that reflect the goodness of God. The business world needs fresh vision from men and women who view their work as a calling from God — bringing the presence of Christ as a businessperson. Whether they're writing emails in cubicles or holding conference calls in C-level suites, businesspeople play a profound role in shaping the future of our world for God's glory.

BEFORE YOU TURN THE PAGE

Reflect

1. How does this view of business compare with how you've previously thought about business?
2. What's the most challenging part of doing business this way?
3. Which story or example connects with you most? Why?
4. How can you begin applying these ideas, either as a consumer or in your work?

Act

1. Go green at the office:
    - Recycle: paper, bottles, packaging.
    - Use recycled materials in your products and office supplies.

- Explore alternative energy sources.
- Use filtered tap water instead of bottled.

2. Establish best practices that reflect the triple bottom line in your hiring, outsourcing, purchasing, marketing, research and development, sales, and so on.
3. Brand yourself with a particular cause (for example, clean water, trafficking, HIV/AIDS), preferably one that aligns with your primary product or service.
4. Become a Stop the Traffik business member: *www.stopthetraffik.org.*
5. Check out the growing Business as Mission movement: *www.businessasmissionnetwork.com.*

CHAPTER 5

TRUE PROGRESS

SCIENCE AND TECHNOLOGY

Which of the following is the best way for a scientist to engage in global mission?

A. Writing a check to support the church's missions program
B. Going on a short-term trip to provide child care for missionaries attending a retreat
C. Finding a cure for HIV
D. Serving on the church missions committee

Fortunately, Christian scientists aren't limited by these four choices. But judging by the rhetoric in many churches, choice C is seldom promoted as a viable option. The application points heard in many sermons are disconnected from our day jobs. Christian scientists should be encouraged and equipped to use their expertise to meet the needs of people. Many scientists are already doing worthwhile work that will drastically benefit the life of the poor and sick. And while nothing should stop them from making donations to charities and going on short-term missions trips, their scientific work may be their greatest contribution to the lasting work of global mission.

The sciences are directly connected to many of the most pressing issues facing our generation. While clean water and medicines are realities most of us take for granted, scientific research is still needed to extend these resources to more people around the world. Science has led to staggering advances in food production, health care, environmental management, and countless other areas. As economist Jeffery Sachs notes, "A special effort of world science, led by global scientific research centers of governments, academic, and industry, must commit specifically to addressing the unmet challenges of the poor."[1]

Our mission with God not only involves people's souls but also includes engaging all of the forces which impinge on our world and make it what it is.[2] The first recorded thing Adam did was scientific — he named the animals (taxonomy). Just a few generations later, Lamech's sons were advancing God's creation by experimenting with the breeding of livestock and making metal (Gen. 4:19 – 22). In this chapter, we'll explore the integral connection between scientific progress and the way we live out our faith, and we'll look at some specific ways research and development can be tapped to respond to the pressing issues of our day.

LIFE-GIVING SCIENCE

The thread that weaves through all the sciences is an interest in studying natural and social phenomenon in order to *sustain life and improve its quality for people near and far.* We need science like we need water and air. Our lives depend on it.

Our increased life expectancy is largely because of scientists who researched the causes behind death, disease, poverty, and hunger. As a result, most of us now enjoy a better quality of life than any civilization preceding ours. Because of scientific research, our generation enjoys better health, higher literacy rates, and better humanitarian practices than ever before in world history. Still, when we watch the evening news, travel overseas, or simply look closely at the lives of those in our neighborhoods and cities, we know that the curse of death and evil has not yet fully been reversed.

Many of our ongoing challenges in the world today require the data, theories, and resulting solutions that come from scientists. Surjit Bhalla, an Indian economist, calculated that the poorest of the poor require nothing more than twenty-nine cents a day to move from complete desperation to a basic, sustainable existence. Twenty-nine cents a day! The answers for closing this gap aren't simple but may well lie in the hands and minds of today's scientists, including economists like Bhalla.[3]

Closer to home, people continue to die from cancer and heart disease, internet chat rooms are destroying marriages, and our oil-dependent lives are wreaking havoc on the planet. Scientists aren't the sole answer to these problems — and sometimes science has even found itself on the wrong side of the problems our world is facing — but scientists can play a significant part in carrying out God's redemptive plan. Raising living standards throughout the world takes several decades. It's not something Western scientists should attempt to do alone, and typically individuals in the developing world should be the driving force behind changes in their own countries. But as noted by best-selling author Gregg Easterbrook, "Building water systems and power plants, sowing high-yield crops.... These are the things that Westerners in general, and Americans in particular, are really good at."[4] Science offers one of the most significant ways for God's hand to reach into society and bring immediate blessing to the lives of people.

FAITH ~~VERSUS~~ SCIENCE

To say Christianity and science have an interesting relationship is an understatement. The two often seem at odds with one another. Whether it's the creation-versus-evolution debate or the ethics of stem cell research and the causes of global warming, evangelicals have often questioned the validity of scientific discoveries and have, at times, been reluctant to embrace the findings of mainstream science.

On the other hand, Western Christians have almost wholeheartedly adopted the scientific method to study the Bible and theology. Bible study methods usually employ the inductive study approach: observe, interpret, apply. And theology is systematized into ten "logical" categories ranging from hamartiology (the study of sin) to eschatology (the study of end times). This is Modern (Theological) Science 101.

We're in desperate need of Christian scientists who intersect their faith with their scientific research and discoveries. Who can help us think Christianly about computer chips and social networking, cloning and Prozac, and hunting and recycling? Without an integration of science and faith, we risk missing the wonders of what we can learn from natural revelation.

In the fifth century, Saint Augustine said that if we interpret the Scriptures without also applying what can be learned from scientific discovery, we *misinterpret* the Bible. In other words, natural inquiry and biblical reflection are both necessary. Several centuries later, Galileo similarly contended that the answers to scientific questions should not be based on Bible reading alone. Christians need to make both natural and biblical observations.[5]

The Bible wasn't written as a scientific textbook, but neither are its principles irrelevant to science. In order to understand the wonders of God's creation, we must not only study the Bible but also engage in conversation and thinking with scientists who offer detailed analysis of elements and compounds, living organisms, stars and planets, and social systems. Christian scientists shouldn't feel that their research somehow plays second fiddle to the work of biblical scholars.[6]

Who will be the next generation of scientists in the universities, in industry, and in government who help us integrate scientific research and development with Christian ideals and biblical principles? How do we ensure that our inventions and discoveries don't run ahead of our ethics, while also continuing to collect and analyze data and construct meaningful solutions to the world's deepest needs? We need to move from simplistic, pious explanations for natural and social phenomena to a more integrated and balanced approach to the tension between faith and science.

THE SEARCH IN RESEARCH

One of the most important ways scientists extend God's reach into the world is through qualitative and quantitative research. Scientists are the ones examining viruses, studying new methods of pollution control, exploring urbanization, investigating cloning and stem cell research, and experimenting with environmentally friendly fertilizers.

We get a good picture of the redemptive value of research through people like Norman Borlaug, whose PhD was in plant pathology and genetics. His research and work saved millions of lives. Early in his career, Borlaug researched ways to develop high-yield, disease-resistant wheat. He eventually introduced his findings to agricultural leaders in Mexico, Pakistan, and India. The wheat yields nearly doubled in these nations, greatly improving food security. Borlaug is often credited with saving over a billion people from starvation, since his research led to a direct increase in the food supply of these impoverished nations. His work offers a compelling example of how research changes people's lives.[7]

Paul Farmer, who is both an anthropologist and a physician, provides another inspiring example of how research can save lives. Farmer has devoted his life to studying the qualitative and quantitative dimensions of infectious diseases. He founded an organization called Partners in Health, which is committed to helping people living in poverty obtain the drugs they need to effectively treat TB and AIDS. His work has particularly helped individuals and communities in Haiti and Peru.[8]

At this point, you may be feeling that individuals like Borlaug and Farmer are among those exceptional few whose work makes a real difference. After all, most scientists probably won't see millions of lives saved directly because of their research. But it's important to remember we can all play a part. These men depended on thousands of other "no-name" scientists who were involved in the research process. Studying cancer cells, analyzing data gathered from victims of sickle-cell anemia, and doing an ethnography in a tribal community are all examples of ways research is being used to respond to global needs.

Jessica was on a short-term missions trip when she discovered firsthand how she could use her love for scientific inquiry to make the world a better place. Like lots of North Americans, Jessica had gone on several short-term missions trips to Mexico as a high school student. Her experiences on those trips made her think seriously about being a missionary to Mexico. She could speak Spanish decently enough, and she had a love for the Mexican people. But when she received a full-ride scholarship to MIT, Jessica decided to pursue an engineering degree. A large chemical company hired her right out of college. She started as a lab researcher in the plastics and rubber division. Although she loved the work she was doing, she sometimes wondered if she had missed her calling, and thought perhaps she should be serving God as a missionary in Mexico. When her church announced an upcoming trip to Mexico City, she jumped at the chance to go back. While on the trip, she noticed an article in the local paper about the increased presence of respiratory problems among people in the community where they were serving. Growing numbers of people in this Mexico City neighborhood were struggling with asthma, chronic bronchitis, and other respiratory ailments. Ironically, Jessica's company had a subsidiary plant nearby, so she strayed from her group for a day to visit the facility. She was appalled when she discovered that her company's plant was using hazardous waste to fuel the production of the materials being manufactured there. And she began to wonder whether there was a connection between the community's increased health issues and her company's production of contaminants. Jessica went on this trip wondering if it might reorient her career toward being a missionary. Instead it started her down an unexpected path: researching the medical implications of the use of alternative fuels in making plastic. As a direct result of Jessica's work, her company recently implemented new regulations forbidding the use of hazardous-waste energy in all their plants.

Researchers may sometimes feel a few steps removed from the front lines of the fight against global problems, but those who are gifted in the sciences need to be given the space and support to do the necessary work that will help improve the quality of life on our planet. Many governments are offering incentives for research that explores effective treatment for neglected diseases like malaria and tuberculosis. The U.S. Food and Drug Administration (FDA) offers priority review for those who develop new drugs for TB. A pharmaceutical company, for example, could simultaneously develop a TB medication *and* a cholesterol-lowering drug. While there isn't much of a financial return to be gained from producing a TB drug, millions of lives could be spared. If produced simultaneously with the TB medication, a cholesterol-lowering drug can bring large financial gains because it meets a growing demand from Westerners. By putting the cholesterol-lowering drug through the review process along with the TB drug, the pharmaceutical company can get both products to the market a year sooner than anticipated, and the profits from the sale of the cholesterol-lowering drug can help fund the development and production of the TB medication.[9]

Research is also needed in the social sciences. Muhammad Yunnus's research as an economist, for example, has improved the quality of life for many of his fellow Bangladeshis. Yunnus studied the cycles of poverty in his homeland of Bangladesh by visiting villages all across the country. One of the first subjects he interviewed was Sufiya Begum, a twenty-one-year-old basket maker and the mother of three children. It cost Sufiya about twenty-two cents to buy the bamboo to make each basket, and she sold them for about twenty-four cents each. She didn't have the money to buy the bamboo directly, so she used middlemen known as the "paikars." She had to sell the baskets back to the paikars at the end of each day in order to repay her loan. Sufiya's profit was just two cents a day per basket. Yunnus began to wonder how her children would break the cycle of poverty.[10] It seemed hopeless to think she could possibly afford to feed and shelter her babies, much less send them to school one day.

Yunnus's research led to the development of Grameen, a bank devoted to providing the poor with small loans. Yunnus knew that simply feeling bad for Sufiya wasn't going to change her situation, but neither would a few bucks to help her through the week! Instead he spent several years researching how to change the systemic cycles that kept millions like Sufiya in a state of poverty. Today more than 250 banking institutions in nearly one hundred countries use the findings of Yunnus's research in their efforts to eradicate poverty through small loans.

Research sometimes gets written off as an ivory-tower pastime that has little real impact on the world. Exploring the relationship between atoms and molecules, researching how to make an affordable antimalaria medicine, and studying the eating habits of African American men is far from impractical. Researchers can use their insights to extend the tangible presence of God's love into the world.

THE ART OF SCIENTIFIC INVENTIONS

In addition to scientists and researchers, we need *engineers* who will work to invent solutions that address the urgent problems of our day. Creating the devices to improve the lifestyle of a quadriplegic, designing furnaces that are more energy efficient, and engineering water filters that can be used in villages in China are a few examples of life-giving inventions.

Robots are no longer limited to science fiction novels. They're used in real-life applications to build cars, harvest crops, help autistic children, and test nuclear equipment. This is a rapidly developing field in great need of robust ingenuity and ethics. One engineer said he initially went into robotics because he thought people would be really impressed. But eventually he began thinking about how to better orient his robotic expertise with his Christian calling. Now he designs robots to dismantle land mines so kids in countries like Afghanistan can play without worrying about getting blown up. Before his robots arrived on the scene, many of the land mines were being dismantled by little kids who were paid next to nothing and often had their hands blown off.[11]

Engineers Without Borders (EWB) is an association that taps this potential by linking engineers with some of the most pressing needs of disadvantaged communities around the world. The New York–based chapter of EWB partnered with a rural community in Cambodia where residents have been dealing with a severe food shortage since an earthen levee was destroyed during the 2000 rainy season. The engineers and local leaders have been collaborating on the design and construction of a twenty-meter water gate and repair of a six-hundred-meter earth embankment in order to provide irrigation water for the community. Once installed, the reservoir will increase the rice crop yield as well as increase the flow of commerce across the river.[12]

There are countless more inventions improving the quality of life for people around the world. Vestergaard Frandsen is a company devoted to producing products that prevent tropical diseases. Among their products are mosquito nets, which help prevent millions of malaria-related deaths, and LifeStraw, a portable water purifier the size of a straw![13] Other engineers and inventors are creating alternative energy solutions, enhancing biochemical safety, designing low-flow toilets and water faucets, and increasing comfort for physically handicapped people.

USE TECHNOLOGY AS A MEANS VERSUS AN END

Technological advances weave through all these scientific domains. And we're in desperate need of researchers and innovators who will help us wrestle with the ethical dimensions of how technology is redefining our understanding of human nature.[14]

We need computer scientists who can blend efficiency, innovation, and ethics with technological expertise. Morally minded specialists in information systems are needed to help us cope with our techno-frenzied lives. I hate to hear computer gurus tell me they feel guilty for not doing something more meaningful in the world. If you decide to uproot from Silicon Valley to start a church in the Middle East, that's great! But please, please, understand our crucial need for Christians with a grasp of these issues who can critically reflect on the missional uses and advancements in technology.

Rick DeVos and Ben Gott tapped the redemptive power of technology when they developed TheCommon.org, a web platform that helps people in communities help each other. DeVos and Gott are passionate about utilizing the web to help people share with one another their needs and abilities. The tool they have developed is especially helpful for megachurches, where congregations are often unaware of the needs and abilities within their own church family. Through TheCommon.org, people can register with their church, post their abilities and resources, and/or list their needs. Then they're connected with other individuals in their church or community who need what they have, or have what they need. DeVos and Gott say, "We're motivated by compassion, care, and facilitating mission-based and charitable works. We seek to be the place on the web where abilities meet needs and needs meet abilities."[15]

MIT professor Nicholas Negroponte's dream is to put a laptop computer into the hands of every child. His vision is for every kid in the world to be given a computer as a means for learning, self-expression, and exploration. He began the One Laptop per Child foundation and created the XO laptop, a computer designed and built specifically for children living in remote areas. It's energy efficient, durable, and the size of a small textbook. It has built-in wireless and a screen that's readable under direct sunlight.[16]

The technology behind social networking, video resources like Ted.com, and high-tech devices to help the physically disabled are filled with life-giving potential. The magnitude of change that has and will occur during our lifetime as a result of technology is staggering. We need to keep a thoughtful eye on the mind-boggling influence of technology in order to channel it for good purposes and subdue its potential evils. Past technologies altered our environment, but many of these new technologies have the potential to change our very souls.[17] This is an issue we will continue to wrestle with in the twenty-first-century world. And we will need technology buffs to help us walk through these challenges and opportunities with wisdom and grace.

COMMISSIONED TO INVESTIGATE

Tim Dearborn of World Vision asks, "How many church mission programs think of computer science and bioengineering projects as suitable domains for Christian mission? How many churches, on a Sunday morning, commission all their members who work professionally in the development of new technologies?"[18] We enthusiastically send our short-term missions teams into the urban slums and lay hands on our elders to commission them for ministry. But science is one of the most life-giving resources available to meet the groans of our world!

Now more than ever, we need to integrate our Christian concerns with new developments in science and technology. Let's stop letting our science run ahead of our ethics and resist feeling threatened in our faith by new scientific discoveries. Science and humanity belong together like dust and Adam.

We were created to live as God's partners in the world, made to explore and study the atoms, bogs, and animals of our world. We need scientists who are willing and ready to accept God's invitation to *investigate* our world. Whether they're in the lab studying germs or in a field planting seeds, scientists play a key role in God's work of returning the world to the way it's meant to be.

BEFORE YOU TURN THE PAGE

Reflect

1. How does this view of science compare with how you've previously thought about science?
2. What's the most challenging part of approaching science and technology this way?
3. Which story or example connects with you most? Why?
4. How can you begin applying these ideas?

Act

1. Partner with relief and development workers, missionaries, and others living in the developing world to learn about the issues facing people who live there.
2. Go on a short-term missions trip to a place where there's a need for someone with your skills. Observe and learn the needs of the community and teach them some basic ways to improve their quality of life.
3. If you're a researcher or an engineer, donate some of your time to work on a neglected issue.
4. Work with gifted communicators to make scientific findings accessible to the rest of us.
5. Help your local church cultivate a theology of science and technology.

CHAPTER 6

THE WORLD IS YOUR CANVAS

ART

I live in the world of words. I spend most of my professional life writing, teaching, and speaking. I journal daily just to stay sane. But there are often moments when I am struck by a particular sentiment or thought that just can't be captured with words. Suddenly I hear Linda practicing a piano concerto in the other room, and it taps something deep within my soul. The music she plays is able to grab my heart and mind in a way that mere words can't. This is the power of art. It has the ability to transcend words. Art helps us celebrate, lament, and discover meaning through our experiences, and it has the capacity to touch us deeply.

Art is a vehicle for worship, and a wonderful form of recreation and enjoyment. It can open up our souls, allowing us to discover and release otherwise untapped potential for creative expression. Art can even be a powerful tool for therapy and can bring about deep healing in the lives of those who have been hurt. We need dancers who display the beauty of Christ in ways that meet the longings of the human spirit and nurture creativity within us. We need films and paintings that make us aware of issues facing the oppressed. We need musical compositions and dramas that inspire us with an imagination for how life is intended to be.

How can Christians express themselves artistically in our modern culture and redeem it as part of God's creation? How can we use the media arts to portray the human condition and to communicate an alternative to the lures of success and wealth? The arts have the capacity for answering pressing questions like: How shall we prepare for the future? And how shall we then live? Art can powerfully influence our view of reality.

In this chapter, we'll explore some of the many ways artists can engage in the issues of our day through their talents and gifts. Even those of us who don't think of ourselves as artists were made to create. We must begin by seeing art as a necessity for our survival and for human flourishing. We'll look at ways to tap the amazing potential of art to make the world a better place and reflect the beauty and glory of God.

ART: LUXURY OR MEANS TO SURVIVAL?

With all the pressing needs in the world, how do we reconcile the importance of art? There have been many inspirational films, performances, and paintings created by artists throughout history in different cultures. But with people dying of hunger and disease, strained school budgets, and raging wars, doesn't art seem like a bourgeois luxury?

Art and creativity are not disposable luxuries. They're core to human survival. Art provides an avenue for us to make sense of our lives and to live out our true identity. Art and creativity tap into something at the very center of our being — the ability to create and the wonder of being cocreators with God.

Travel back with me to World War II for a moment. The year is 1940, and France has recently joined the war against Nazi Germany. Oliver Messiaen, one of France's rising young composers, has been captured by Nazi soldiers and dragged away to a concentration camp. Like most of his fellow prisoners, Messiaen lives in squalid conditions, and his days are spent looking for food and water, doing forced labor, and trying to escape the next beating. While in the camp, he's inspired by reading Revelation 10, where the apostle John describes the trumpet sound of the seventh angel. John paints a vivid picture of the consummation of the mysteries of God, and Messiaen is inspired to compose music. His experience of reading the Scriptures in the midst of these horrid conditions led to his famed composition Quartet for the End of Time. He knew of three other musicians in the camp with him—a clarinetist, cellist, and violinist—and Messiaen wrote the piece with them in mind. His masterpiece was first played for the four thousand prisoners and guards in the prison camp where he was confined.

Concentration camps hardly seem like the ideal conditions for inspiring a great work of music. Yet Messiaen's story is by no means unique. There is an abundance of poetry, literature, music, and visual art created by other prisoners living in Nazi concentration camps. At a time when survival was their primary objective, people living in these difficult circumstances discovered that art was a necessity for survival. The camps were places without money, commerce, recreation, or basic respect—but the prisoners still had the ability to create. Art is a part of our calling, and creating it is essential to our survival. It is a core expression of the human spirit, one of the many ways we declare, "I am alive!"[1]

Karl Paulnack, director of the Boston Conservatory of Music, was living in Manhattan on 9/11. He describes what it was like to sit down at his piano for a practice session on September 12, 2001: "I did it by force of habit, without thinking about it. I lifted the cover on the keyboard, and opened my music, and put my hands on the keys and took my hands off the keys. And I sat there and thought, does this even matter? Isn't this completely irrelevant? Playing the piano right now, given what happened in this city yesterday, seems silly, absurd, irreverent, and pointless. Why am I here? What place has a musician in this moment in time? Who needs a piano player right now? I was completely lost."[2]

Instead of practicing, Paulnack went for a walk around his Manhattan neighborhood. One of the first things he noticed was people singing. Some were standing outside firehouses singing "We Shall Overcome," and others were circled together in groups singing "America the Beautiful." As he remembers that somber week, Paulnack recalls the first public gathering in New York after the attacks — a New York Philharmonic performance of Brahms' *Requiem*. He says, "The first organized public expression of grief, our first communal response to that historic event, was a concert. That was the beginning of a sense that life might go on. The U.S. military secured the airspace, but recovery was led by the arts, and by music in particular, that very night."[3]

Art has the power to bring hope, redemption, and meaning to shattered lives. Of course, that same capability can also be used to destroy hope and to create disillusionment and heartache. Art is so much more than mindless entertainment. Even art that doesn't appeal to our tastes is frequently a cry from the soul. What's the story behind the nineteenth-century impressionist art hanging on our wall? What cries of lament are pounding through the vibrating rap music playing in the car driving by us?[4] When you encounter someone's artwork, be attuned to the human cry for survival.

USE YOUR PLATFORM

Every artist has a different platform from which to shape the world. Independent film festivals, YouTube, and blockbuster Hollywood epics are all platforms that can be used to bring healing to our broken world through film. Some people make their greatest artistic contribution by teaching seven-year-olds in a private studio, while others do so from Carnegie Hall and the Met. From sketch pads, art studios, and murals to poems, novels, blueprints, and gardens, the platforms for art in the twenty-first-century world are expanding every day. The challenge for artists is to determine which platform best suits their passion and desire to contribute to the world's needs, while remaining faithful to the platforms they've been given by God. Many artists hope to break out and make it big, but most are called to faithfully create their art in smaller venues, making a difference one life at a time.

That said, there are plenty of artists who have made it big and are using their fame to make a difference. Actors like Morgan Freeman, musicians like Piotr Anderszewski, and novelists like Barbara Kingsolver hold the attention of millions. The work of these individuals can bring healing to lives through the power of art. Many famous artists are also using their notoriety to direct attention to important causes in the world. Bono, Cameron Diaz, Brad Pitt, and Penelope Cruz are among several celebrities who have used their Hollywood platform to support the One campaign, a global effort to reduce poverty. Brad Pitt says, "I can't get out of the press. These [Africans] can't get in the press. So let's redirect the attention a little bit. It drives me mental seeing what I've seen and knowing that it doesn't show up in our news every day. I mean, literally thousands of people died today."[5] Many have questioned Pitt's and Angelina Jolie's motives for their international adoptions, advocacy efforts for the poor, and attempts to rebuild New Orleans. But I'm still thankful for their desire to redirect the limelight from their stage to the global issues that matter to them.

What about the rest of us? Most of us probably aren't being chased by the paparazzi. What does it mean for independent artists to use their platforms to honor God? First, in an age of technologically fueled globalization, don't discount how quickly you can find yourself on a *global* platform. What you intend to simply be viewed or listened to by some friends or followers could easily be picked up by someone from another part of the world. Where is the next generation of artists who will tap internet-based platforms to highlight some of the pressing issues of our day?

More important, don't discount the platform you have right now. Most people in the world won't visit a symphony hall or famous art gallery anytime soon, but people all over continue to hear live music at clubs, coffeehouses, and even in churches. People in your neighborhood will see art hanging in local restaurants and stores. Friends can be encouraged by a poem you write for them. Every artist has a platform, even if it's as simple as painting a picture for a friend or teaching guitar to a neighbor. The goal isn't necessarily to create an internationally acclaimed masterpiece; it's about being faithful with the platforms you're given and doing what you were made to do—create—in a way that honors God. Trust God to determine where you can make your best artistic contribution in the world.

CHRISTIAN VERSUS "SECULAR" ART

There are many ways for us to get involved artistically as Christians. Too often we simply copy mainstream culture and put a Christian label on it. To the artists reading this: please, please, please, don't contribute to the long line of cheesy Christian books, movies, and music that display anything *but* the excellencies of Jesus. Perhaps sitcom character Hank Hill in *King of the Hill* sizes it up best when he decides he's had enough of Christian rock music and declares, "You're not making Christianity better. You're making rock 'n' roll worse!"[6]

If we encounter artwork that is degrading, unhelpful, or downright evil, the best Christian response isn't to make a sanitized Christian version of it. Crowd it out by making something better![7] Some Christian artists may believe the best way to do this is by creating art with messages and ideas that are explicitly Christian. I welcome that. But we desperately need Christians who contribute artistically in broader contexts of society too.

Isaac Slade, lead singer and pianist of the Fray, describes what it was like for him to suddenly realize that his purely Christian lyrics made no sense to his friends outside the church. They didn't even get what the songs were about. Slade says, "I'm a musician. This is my job.... If you're a painter, paint, but you don't have to have Jesus in every picture. Paint well, and if you paint well enough, they might ask you why you do that."[8]

Ask yourself: What does Jesus look like in the form of an artist? How does my art illuminate Christ in unexplored ways? How might the world best encounter who Jesus is and what he's about through art? Who will be the "priestly" artists working in Hollywood studios, Juilliard classrooms, and architectural firms, creating excellent work under the lordship of Jesus? We need Christian artists who talk with their colleagues about Jesus, practice earth-friendly artistry, raise the bar for excellence, and promote themes that reflect the concerns of Christ.

PAINTING THE FACELESS

Another way artists can partner with God is by giving a face to the faceless. One time when I was visiting China, I went with a physician to a leprosy village. After several hours treating the people there, the doctor asked, "Why doesn't anyone here have a mirror?" They responded, "Whenever people look at us, they turn away. So we're afraid to see what we look like." Sadly, while the rich and famous can't get out of the spotlight, many of the most oppressed people on earth remain faceless, hidden to most of society. Artists have a unique opportunity to paint the faceless and help us see these "invisible" people.

One way to help the invisible is to take the Brad Pitt approach—redirecting the spotlight to those who aren't seen and lack a platform to speak for themselves. Another approach is to center the artwork on the faceless themselves. Ben Affleck was gripped by the plight of Congolese refugees, and he made a short film called *Gimme Shelter*. The film tells of displaced Congolese families who fled conflict and are now living under makeshift shelter. He used his gifts in acting and production to make a film that brought attention to these oppressed people.[9]

Again, I realize most of us don't have the notoriety or resources of Pitt or Affleck, but consider the example of Sarah Wolfe. I met Sarah a couple years ago when I was speaking at her church in Boston. Her day job is working as a caseworker with HomeStart, a nonprofit organization that deals with homelessness in Boston. The homeless people with whom Sarah works are not simply clients or projects to her; they're her friends. One day while she was thinking about what these dear homeless friends mean to her and to Jesus, she decided to pull out her paintbrush and palette. She painted a crucifixion scene with her homeless friends at the foot of the cross (see photo). Park Street Church in Boston displayed the painting in their building for several months, and the painting impacted both the congregation who attend there and the homeless who live nearby. Sarah told me, "My clients are very poor. Some are mentally ill, level-three sex offenders, robbers, prostitutes, or drug addicts. These are the people I love to paint, because

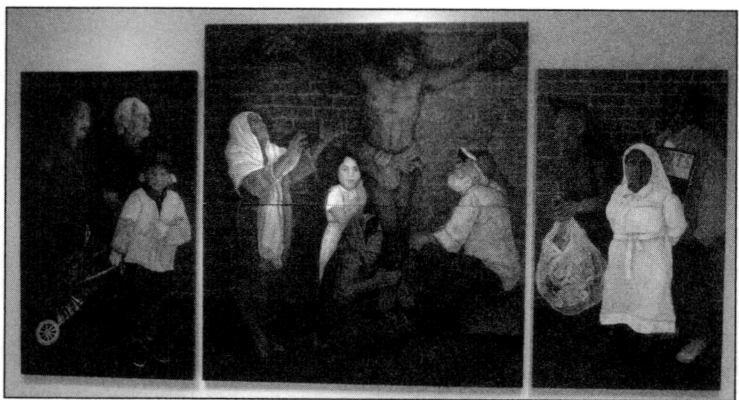

The Crucifixion, Sarah Wolfe's portrayal of Christ and her homeless friends

I know Jesus loves them so much." Sarah is living out her priestly role by painting the faceless.

Beverly Collins is a painter with a similar passion. She wanted to elevate people's awareness of the Sudan crisis, so she started painting images of Darfuri women. She wanted people to see the hurt and atrocities they were suffering. Collins' exhibit The Invisible Women of Darfur makes these otherwise "invisible" women visible to those of us who live a world away.[10]

A word of caution is in order here. In our attempts to give a face to the faceless, we need to do so in a way that offers them dignity and respect. This is one of the things I really appreciate about Sarah. Her primary intent in her art isn't to emphasize the distraught conditions of her homeless friends. Instead she wants to portray them as image bearers of God, loved and cared for by Jesus. Other artists share a similar concern. The primary goal of Alejandro Monteverde, the director of the hit movie *Bella,* is to portray positive models of Latinos on the screen in order to counter the many disparaging images that are often portrayed in film and media. In our noble attempts to open eyes to the lives and circumstances of the oppressed, we must be careful to do it in a humanizing, honoring way—lest we perpetuate the very oppression we're trying to subvert.

Examples abound of Christian artists who are giving a face to the faceless and a voice to the voiceless. Stephen Curtis Chapman writes and performs songs about orphans and has personally adopted children. Three California guys have used their passion for film-making to visualize child soldiers in Uganda through their well-known documentary called *Invisible Children*. Millions of artists write songs, design websites, and create poems to help us see the faceless. The old cliché is still true: a picture is worth a thousand words. And the pictures artists create give the world a powerful lens to examine the global issues we care about so deeply.

EXPOSING EVIL

Art can also powerfully expose the evils that bedevil our time. There is a place for thoughtfully and wisely exposing the atrocities and despair that can sometimes remain hidden. Zana Briski, a New York–based photographer, spent some extended time in the red-light district of Calcutta with women working in prostitution. Zana taught the children of these women how to use a camera, and she used the pictures they took to expose people to the horrible conditions of life in the sex industry in Calcutta. There are many redemptive layers to Briski's project. Her work with the kids offered them a therapeutic outlet, which allowed them a chance to see the world through a different lens. She also arranged for several of the children to attend a boarding school where they would be safer and could receive a quality education. And many people around the world were alerted to sex trafficking in Calcutta and other places through Briski's documentary, *Born into Brothels*.[11]

Several artists have used art to expose the evils of the genocide in Sudan. Award-winning novelist David Eggers teamed up with a Sudanese refugee to write one of the most moving novels I've read in a long time. His book *What Is the What* is a visceral account of the barbaric quality of life of those who lived through the long war in Sudan. And Emmanuel Jal is a hip-hop artist who sings on stages around the world to expose people to the evils of what he experienced as a child soldier in Sudan. By age thirteen, Jal had already fought in two civil wars and was so close to starvation that he considered eating one of his fallen comrades. He was rescued by a British aid worker who raised him in Nairobi, but the scars of being a child solider continued to eat away at his soul. Jal started singing as a way to ease and heal his pain. After a while, he found that he couldn't stop singing. And he still can't. Now he's exposing the savage treatment of people in Sudan to the global community. There are other places around the world facing similar atrocities, and more artists are needed who will work to expose these evils. Art like this has the power to awaken people across the globe to do something that will end the evils of genocide, disease, poverty, and human greed.

One of my favorite journalists is the provocative *New York Times* columnist Nicholas Kristof. He uses the art of writing to expose evil and provoke people to grapple with complex issues. Kristof's travels have taken him around the world, where he's done extensive reporting on the sex industry, child labor, and sweatshops. His widely read column forces his readers to pay attention to issues and topics they would normally never think about. "I believe that once Americans pay attention, they'll get upset and the political process will work and politicians will respond," Kristof says. "This is not just a journalistic or literary exercise; I write the columns because I want to make a difference."[12]

Novels, memoirs, and movies are some of the most compelling ways to awaken society to evil in our world. The movie *Kite Runner* exposes the heartache of life in Afghanistan, *Hotel Rwanda* is a heart-wrenching portrayal of genocide, and films like *Crash* and *Man Gone Down* visualize the incredibly tension-packed nature of race relations in the United States.

When Terry George wrote and directed *Hotel Rwanda*, he said, "It's a story that will take cinema-goers around the world inside an event that, to all our great shame, we knew nothing about. But more than that, it will allow audiences to join in the love, the loss, the fear and the courage of a man who could have been any of us."[13] This inside look at the genocide in Rwanda brought audiences to their knees (including Linda and me!). And it had a profound impact on the actors themselves. Don Cheadle was so deeply moved through his work in the movie that he has now become a leading advocate to prevent Rwandan-like genocides from happening elsewhere.

Art is a powerful way to "speak up for those who cannot speak for themselves" (Prov. 31:8). What evils and issues tug most on your heart? How can you use art as a way to expose those evils before society at large?

SUPPORTING THE ARTS

I don't really think of myself as an artist. Sure—my writing is a creative outlet for me, and I spent time studying music in high school and college. But my family and friends go running the other way when we're pairing up to play Pictionary. Still, art is a big part of my life. As a leader, writer, and father, I want to inspire, shape, and support those who are gifted in the arts. My girls love to paint, draw, sculpt, sing, and dance. I applaud their growth in these pursuits, and I get a wonderful glimpse into their concerns and interests through their art. I stop Linda when she starts to berate her degrees in piano performance as an impractical waste of time and money. As a family, we support local bands and catch the symphony and ballet whenever we can. The true value of art can't always be quantified by numbers and outcomes. It's a privilege and responsibility to support the arts, because they tap into our core identity as cocreators with God and they allow us to experience the radiant beauty of God's creation.

There are a variety of ways those of us who are less artistically inclined can think about supporting the arts. Our friends Andrew and Lynn Rudd live on a modest income, but they've made a commitment to budget one thousand dollars each year to buy art for their home. Their house is filled with an amazing display of art from many different artists. Another friend makes sure she never misses a neighbor's piano recital, and one of my colleagues supports the arts by only using marketing images for her business that have been created by local artists.

Growing numbers of churches are also supporting the arts and incorporating them into the ministry of the church. In many churches, it's become common to see painters working on a picture during a sermon, and walls covered with paper where people are encouraged to worship through drawing.

One of the best ways to support the arts is by molding and shaping other artists. I love eavesdropping on Linda while she teaches piano. She believes there's something sacred about teaching students five-finger patterns and scales to help them discover the magic of playing a simple melody. She's heard so many stories about adults who quit piano lessons as kids because of their "mean piano teacher." Consequently, one of Linda's primary motivations as a piano teacher is to give her students a real love for music. Even if they never go near a keyboard as an adult, she wants them to tap into the life-giving wonder of music. I married an amazing woman and artist!

Crystal VanHekken went to college to be a pediatrician. But she quickly discovered she wasn't wired for the sciences. While fulfilling an art requirement, she fell in love with the world of dance. Some people thought she was crazy to quit her pre-med studies to embrace a future as a starving artist. But Crystal, now a dance teacher in a public high school, loves every minute of what she does as she introduces students to the wonder and beauty of dance.

Pam (not her real name) is another artist actively supporting the arts. She's a Christian artist from Boston who lives in China and runs an art gallery. Her gallery isn't a front to do missions work. In a culture where sciences and manufacturing are highly regarded, Pam is in China to help redeem the arts and increase their visibility. For her, this means wrestling with the question, What would the arts look like if sin had never entered the world? Pam's gallery regularly exhibits Chinese artwork and hosts lectures, film nights, and concerts. Her aim is to display art that celebrates beauty and goodness. She looks for pieces that offer hope amid the disillusionment, cynicism, and sense of meaninglessness often felt by many modern Chinese. Pam also works with other Chinese artists to bring hope to the marginalized in their society. Together they offer art education and opportunities to millions in migrant communities across the country. In Pam's words, "Why do I do this? Because everything matters!"—including art!

DRINK IN THE BEAUTY

The artistic beauty of our Creator abounds in every corner of the earth. God created us to enjoy and be moved by the power of art, from the soaring pines of the forest to the white surf of the ocean, from brilliant marigolds to gray storm clouds. And that same power can be tapped and directed to meet some of the deepest needs of our world.

Whether art is a career for you, just a hobby, or a cause you support, look for ways to more intentionally direct art to partner with God in making the world a better place. In the words of Boston Conservatory director Karl Paulnack, "Music is one of the ways we make sense of our lives, one of the ways in which we express feelings when we have no words, a way for us to understand things with our hearts when we cannot with our minds. Someday someone is going to walk into your concert hall and bring you a mind that is confused, a heart that is overwhelmed, a soul that is weary. Whether they go out whole again will depend partly on how well you do your craft."[14]

His words apply equally to painters, sculptors, architects, dancers, writers, and the many other artists in the world. Or in the words of famed novelist Stephen King, "Writing is magic, as much the water of life as any other creative art. The water is free. So drink. Drink and be filled up."[15] Sip the life-giving water of God's creation through art, and share it with those around you.

BEFORE YOU TURN THE PAGE

Reflect

1. How does this view of the arts compare with how you've previously thought about them?
2. What's the most challenging part of approaching the arts with this mindset?
3. Which story or example connects with you most? Why?
4. As a consumer of art or as an artist, how can you begin applying these ideas?

Act

1. Choose an issue or cause around which to orient your art.
2. If you teach others, offer reduced or pro bono lessons to a couple students in an underprivileged community.
3. Use environmentally friendly tools (paints, sound, and so on).

4. Put on a benefit show and donate the proceeds to a cause.
5. Collaborate with other artists to study a global issue together and develop an artistic response.

CHAPTER 7

URGENT CARE

HEALTH CARE AND WELLNESS

I just got back from my morning run. I love to run. It's not because I'll be breaking any competitive records. But it's therapeutic to my body, soul, and spirit. I haven't spent any time studying or working in the field of health care. But I'm grateful for the many doctors, counselors, and coaches who have helped me care for my body and my health. Running regularly helps me fight the chronic heart disease that has plagued my mother's side of my family for generations. It frees my mind from the constant onslaught of emails pinging for my attention. Running is a deeply spiritual ritual for me.

This chapter is about caring for ourselves and caring for others, two interconnected ideas. To care for others, we must care for ourselves, or we won't have much to offer them! Caring for others necessarily includes our own self-care. We'll also consider what it means to eat, live, drink, sleep, and exercise in a way that honors our image-bearing gift. And we'll talk about caring for the health and well-being of others. We'll deal with these as interdependent priorities throughout the chapter.

Specifically, we'll encounter nurses, counselors, physicians, and athletes who are living out their priestly calling by bringing the healing presence of Jesus to care for the minds and bodies of other people. Including these varied professions in the same chapter aligns with a larger movement toward holistic care that has been happening in medical schools and hospitals over the last couple decades. This movement attends to the relationship between mental health and physical well-being.

How does a nurse caring for a patient with a terminal prognosis partner with God? What about a physician treating children with malaria? How does God work through a counselor or a physical therapist? And how should our partnership with God shape the way we eat, sleep, and exercise? Care, wisdom, and compassion are needed in all these areas.

TAKE AS DIRECTED

My grandfather died of a heart attack on a Toronto streetcar. My mom's family knew he had heart problems, but the only treatment in his era was to pop a nitro pill in his mouth to reduce some of the annoying symptoms. My mother has outlived her dad—both in the number of years she's lived *and* in the number of heart attacks she's survived! Because of stents, balloons, and other technologies, my mom continues to bless us with her life. The advances that have been made in medical treatment are one of the amazing wonders of our lifetime.

Just a hundred years ago, the average American lived to be forty-one years old. In 1928, futurists predicted that life expectancy might someday reach sixty-five. The U.S. Social Security system was built on the premise that most people would retire at sixty-five, and the majority would never live long enough to receive more than a couple of benefit checks. Today the average life expectancy of North Americans is seventy-seven years. In fact, the worldwide life expectancy is up to sixty-six. People are living both longer and healthier than ever before.[1]

Doctors and nurses are often told that serving on missions trips and supporting others who go overseas is the best way they can respond to the needs of the world. But the most important contribution health care professionals can make to the world is to *provide excellent health care for the body, soul, and spirit.*

As people live longer and as life becomes increasingly frenetic, holistic care is needed for growing numbers of people. Nothing more tangibly demonstrates the healing, redemptive power of God's reign than bringing healing to the mind and body. We should continue to pray for God's miraculous healing, and sometimes God supernaturally provides that through prayer and faith alone. But we should also be grateful for the miracle of God's extended hand caring for people through medical treatment. God uses hospital personnel to care for the sick and hurting. He uses dentists, nurse practitioners, lab technicians, and physical therapists to bring treatment, relief, and comfort to millions of people.

Diagnosis and Treatment

Health care professionals have two primary goals: diagnosis and treatment. Given the insane demands placed on many doctors today, diagnosis is often done somewhat haphazardly, without a good understanding of what's behind the symptoms. Being God's partner in the examining room begins with slowing down to listen to patients and family members so you can offer a good diagnosis. Social workers, nurses, and office personnel can help doctors with this task by talking with patients as they record vital signs and symptoms and doing so with respect and care. The charting that consumes the life of a nurse has redemptive value!

Accurate diagnosis relies upon ongoing learning and research. Understanding the latest findings of medical research is far above my pay grade, but I'm grateful that my doctor is up on the recent discoveries and controversies related to antibiotics and alternative medicine. Medical professionals need to be highly observant of patterns of diseases and alert to recurring responses to medications and manipulative procedures.[2] Listening to the family circumstances of a patient, their work situation, and their personal anxieties can provide important insights. Redemptive health care begins with accurate diagnosis, which comes from good listening. And a diagnosis delivered compassionately can help relieve a patient's anxiety about an unknown illness or injury.

The second goal is treatment, which may include finding a cure, relieving suffering, offering rehabilitative procedures, or preventing future illness. Prayerfully administered treatments should be well researched and clearly communicated to patients and family members. Patients facing a permanent disability need treatment that is both medically sound and compassionate, helping them live as closely as possible to God's intended design despite their disability.

Christian health care professionals need both the medical community *and* their churches to help them discern the most appropriate treatment for a patient with a terminal prognosis. When should a nurse move from praying for recovery to praying for peace, acceptance, and the grace to die well? When does a doctor move from aggressive medical intervention to assuring a patient and family of comfort and minimal pain in dying?[3] As health care workers wrestle with these questions, they're living out their priestly calling.

Bedside Manner

Both diagnosis and treatment need to be done in a way that exemplifies the loving care of God's healing hand. Hospitals can be scary places. When a nurse spends an extra few minutes listening and talking, it goes a long way with patients and their families. Family members often feel helpless watching a stranger feed and bathe their loved one. There's something deeply unnerving for a mom to see people wake up her sleeping son to take his blood pressure, check his pulse rate, and count respirations. Add to this the anxiety of the unknown. A caring look, a word of encouragement, and an effort to clearly explain what's going on are some practical ways to help people encounter Christ's presence in the midst of diagnosis and treatment.

The importance of this kind of bedside manner is heightened when dealing with patients and families who are far away from home. I experienced this firsthand when I was in a dune buggy accident in Brazil. I suffered numerous internal injuries, including a ruptured spleen. On top of the excruciating pain was the added disorientation of how things worked in a Brazilian hospital. I was really grateful for "Aunt Amy," a missionary nurse who not only interpreted between the doctors and me but also took time to explain what was happening.

When giving treatment and care to a newly arrived immigrant or a refugee family, be extra attentive. Medical jargon sounds foreign to most of us, but it sounds especially alien to those for whom English is a second language. If you treat people from a different culture, I highly recommend you read Anne Fadiman's book *The Spirit Catches You and You Fall Down*, a heart-wrenching story of a Hmong family trying to care for their epileptic daughter in Merced, California.

Only God performs miracles. But he often does so through the hands of a loving nurse and a careful surgeon. When health care professionals help eliminate extensive suffering and increase the longevity and quality of life, this is part of God's miraculous work in the world. Health care professionals have unique opportunities to serve where they work and to share Christ's love by the way they care for the sick and their loved ones.

IT'S ALL IN YOUR HEAD

Think of the last time you had a headache. Chances are, the muscles in your head and the chemicals in your brain were responding to stress. Research, not to mention our own experience, shows us a clear link between our mental and physical health. Many of the things we've already discussed, including the importance of accurate diagnosis, proper treatment and a caring bedside manner, apply to the mental health field as well. Counselors should recognize the importance of initial meetings with clients and learn to accurately assess, diagnose, and treat them.

Individuals working in either the mental or physical health professions need to appreciate the symbiotic nature of our minds and our bodies. Forty-three percent of North American adults suffer adverse health effects from stress, and 75 percent to 90 percent of all physician office visits are for stress-related ailments and complaints. Stress is linked to the six leading causes of death: heart disease, cancer, lung ailments, accidents, cirrhosis of the liver, and suicide.[4] Growing numbers of studies demonstrate a correlation between depression and people's susceptibility to disease. People with serious mental illness have higher rates of grave medical illness and premature death than the general population.[5] Despite our increased life span and technological conveniences, we're more stressed out than ever before.

It takes very little imagination to see the opportunities for mental health professionals to partner with God in their work. Offering hope, counseling, and treatment can be powerful tools of redemption. Social workers, counselors, psychiatrists, and psychologists are needed who have a strong belief in the uniqueness, sanctity, and beauty of each individual life. Whether we are helping someone work through depression, deal with a strained marriage, overcome addictions, or live with an ongoing mental disorder, God needs individuals who are committed to healing the ravaging effects of sin on our minds.

Sue VanWyngarden's Christian faith informs the way she approaches the clients she counsels. When helping someone with depression, anxiety, or a battle with addiction, she uses typical strategies like cognitive, behavioral therapy, and stress-coping mechanisms. But she remains continually aware that there's a spiritual dimension involved in these battles as well. She doesn't prey on a client's emotional vulnerability, but she does pray for them! Sue is convinced prayer is a powerful tool that remains untapped by far too many counselors. Prayer, stress-coping strategies, and retelling our story are *all* deeply spiritual approaches to mental health.

CARING FOR THE UNDERDOG

Conditions like schizophrenia, cancer, and AIDS afflict rich and poor alike. God needs health care professionals to extend Christ's care to people, wherever they live, whatever their circumstances. The Scriptures remind us that God consistently acts on behalf of the underdog and that God's ear is tuned to the cry of the oppressed. Many health care professionals have found creative ways to offer treatment to the underdogs of today's world.

In 1992, Dr. Rob Cheeley left his home state of Idaho to begin a cooperative effort with the Yunnan Provincial Bureau of Health in China to train village doctors. When Rob first arrived, the medical and dental care for the poor living in Yunnan was bleak. So

Rob began recruiting other medical professionals to join him in his efforts and soon established projects all throughout the region to train village doctors and provide free treatment to the minority people of Southwest China. Rob now leads an organization in China with about 250 Christian professionals — both expatriates and indigenous Chinese. Several thousand patients are treated each year, including those suffering from leprosy, babies with cleft palates (who may otherwise be thrown in the dump), and disabled people needing physical therapy. Rob is one of many medical professionals who believe that the best way to serve God is to spend your life offering the tangible compassion of Jesus to people struggling to survive, by caring for their physical ailments and pains.

Most Christian health care workers choose to remain closer to home. The Christian Medical and Dental Association (CMDA) has developed a simple model to help doctors incorporate treatment for underprivileged people as part of their ongoing work. CMDA challenges its members to give at least 4 percent of their money or time to the needs of the poor. Those who volunteer their time might choose to go overseas for two weeks to share their medical expertise, or offer to see one uninsured patient for every twenty-five paying ones. They might volunteer one night a month at a local clinic for patients who can't pay, as well as the growing number of Medicaid patients being served.

For health care workers who decide to give their 4 percent overseas, the options are endless. Local health workers want teaching about internal and general medicine, pediatrics, obstetrics, dentistry, and burn care. Victims of human trafficking are in need of psychologists who are willing to help them work through fear and trauma. People with infected gums and rotting teeth need dental treatment. Groups like Doctors Without Borders and Partners in Health exist primarily to connect medical professionals with opportunities like these.

Other doctors volunteer their time to care for the poor in their own communities. Tandy Champion runs an internal medicine and pediatric practice. After finishing residency, she set up her practice so she could be in the office three days a week, keeping two days a week open for voluntary medical work and serving in her local church. Initially,

Tandy thought she'd slowly transition to this new schedule after building a successful practice, but she was soon convinced there was no better time than the present to get started helping others! Tandy was also instrumental in helping start Health Intervention Services (HIS), a nonprofit health care center for the uninsured and working poor.

Jodi Boyd treats underprivileged people at home and overseas. She recently sold her house and became a traveling nurse. She takes on thirteen-week assignments in the United States in places where there's a desperate need for interim nursing care. This program covers her room and board, and she saves the remaining income to spend her alternate quarters nursing overseas. Jodi recently spent three months in Pakistan and then the next three in Maine. She lived for three months on a refitted cruise ship, serving with Mercy Ships in Liberia, and then spent the next three working in northern California. Nurses like her are changing the world by treating people with care and compassion, both near and far. This is how we were created to live!

A word of caution is in order here. Anytime we start using a skill in another cultural context, we need to do a little homework first. Even when we're diagnosing people here in the United States, it's important

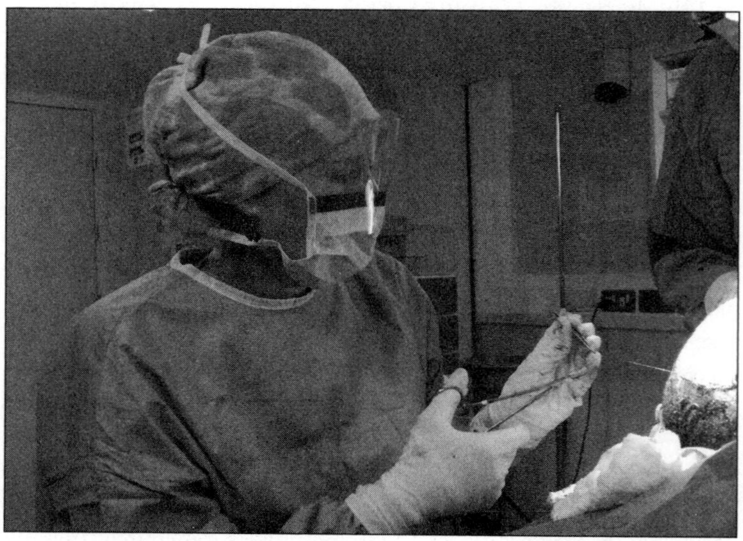

Jodi Boyd treating a patient in Liberia

that we take the time to understand the specific context and circumstances behind the ailment or problem before we start diagnosing and prescribing solutions. When practiced with wisdom and sensitivity to the unique situation of each individual, the act of healing, providing treatment, and relieving suffering powerfully expresses God's care for the underdogs of society, in a way that few things can.

PREVENTION OVER TREATMENT

Preventative health has become a growing industry and field of research. Hospitals are now opening fitness centers, and insurance companies are offering reduced rates for clients who practice healthy habits. Growing numbers of experts in the field of international development and medical researchers believe that preventative approaches to disease should be *prioritized* above treating those who have disease. Let's look at this new area of care in two different contexts—AIDS and athletics/fitness.

HIV/AIDS

The HIV/AIDS pandemic offers a good case study for understanding the pros and cons of prevention versus treatment. Some international development experts argue that the compassionate initiatives used to treat AIDS victims may be costing more lives than they save. Over the last several years, the United States has increased funding for HIV/AIDS initiatives around the world but has cut money for children's health care and other global priorities by nearly a hundred million dollars![6] While we certainly can't reduce these issues to mere economics, it is helpful to note that preserving life through the prevention of AIDS, malaria, and tuberculosis costs far less than treating people with those illnesses. Economist William Easterly claims, "For the same money spent giving one more year of life to an AIDS patient, you could give 75 to 1,500 years of additional life ... to the rest of the population through AIDS prevention" (for example, fifteen extra years for five to one hundred people).[7]

Uganda is a powerful example of what *can* happen when prevention is prioritized. In 1988, Uganda was named the epicenter of the AIDS crisis, with 26 percent of the adult population infected. That was the highest percentage known of any country in the world at that point. It was impossible to keep up with treating the sick. The percentages of infected and dying people were growing, and without a drastic intervention, the entire nation would be annihilated.

Government officials, researchers, and charitable organizations put their heads together to come up with a solution for the pandemic threatening to wipe out Uganda. They developed a values-based prevention program widely known today as the ABC approach to HIV/AIDS.

A = Abstinence (from sex outside of marriage)
B = Be faithful (to your spouse)
C = Condoms (when all else fails or when you decide you "can't" be faithful)

A and B were taught as the most viable ways of preventing HIV/AIDS for both single and married adults. But a condom-distribution program was also developed, because it was known that some citizens would shrug off abstinence and monogamous sex as unrealistic. What happened? Uganda moved from being the epicenter of AIDS in 1988 to being the least infected country in Sub-Saharan Africa fifteen years later. Here are the numbers:

- In 1988, 26 percent of Ugandan adults were HIV/AIDS positive.
- In 2003, 4 percent of Ugandan adults were HIV/AIDS positive.

Uganda learned the strategic value of preventative health. In fact, the Chinese government later asked the Ugandan government to describe for them how they implemented their preventative plan. The Ugandan officials replied, "We tapped into the most grassroots organization available to us all throughout the country—Christian churches. They exist in every city, town, and village. The churches learned the program and became educational centers for teaching the ABC approach." What a beautiful picture of the church living out her God-given role to be the hands and feet of Jesus in the world!

Athletics and Fitness

It's easy to understand the value of preventative health for people living in villages in Uganda and China. When people learn to separate their waste from their drinking water and heed warnings about polygamous sex, it sustains life. But Americans can also use a good dose of preventative health care! The medical advances that have helped to extend our lives are now being reversed by our frenzied, high-fat lifestyles. More than half the U.S. population are overweight, eating high-fat diets and not getting enough sleep each night. My mother's life has been sustained through advanced treatment of heart disease. But I want more than good treatment for me. I want to change my family's history of heart disease by making lifestyle decisions that will prevent it from affecting my kids and me. I'm well aware that fit, health-conscious runners can still die early from a heart attack. But healthy eating and exercise *can* reduce my chances of a heart attack—and that's something that lies in my power to change.

Physical education majors often get a bum rap in college for pursuing a lightweight degree. But we need to redeem our understanding of the importance of play and fitness, powerful tools for preventative health. Caring for our bodies in the way we eat, exercise, sleep, and play is closely connected to our ability to live as God intends. Whether it's a serious workout at the gym, a game of tag with our kids, or a brisk walk in the fresh air, physical exercise and play have the power to release many of the tensions we carry with us in our fast-paced lives. Sports and fitness also have the potential to test our self-control, honesty, perseverance, concentration, intelligence, and skillfulness and help us build a connection to others in our community. We need Christians who are gifted to motivate and equip the rest of us to engage in sports and play to those ends. Our lives may depend on it!

Even professional athletes can direct their work and influence to making the world a better place. Aaron Kampman is one of the Green Bay Packers' most community- and global-minded players. Early in his career, Aaron spoke regularly at schools and youth groups, visited kids in the hospital, and distributed food to needy families in Green Bay. Now Aaron and his wife are likely to be found in India and Kenya during the off-season, scouting out ways to invest their time, abilities, and money. Aaron is using his growing influence and his athletic skills to help people living in extreme poverty meet Jesus. He invites other athletes to join him in using their abilities and platforms to teach those living in poverty about discipline, teamwork, selflessness, health, and most of all, the love of Christ. He wants to use his experience with sports to find ways of meeting people's pressing needs. Aaron is a living picture of Jesus both in the NFL and in poor villages across the world.

Whether it's in the NFL or in the local community Little League, athletic involvement usually involves serious competition. Competitive sport can bring out the best and the worst in us, depending on how it's directed and how we choose to respond to victories, losses, and the pressure to win. Christian athletes and trainers are needed who can help channel this competitive energy in ways that build godly character and model the fruit of God's Spirit. Bringing our best to our game and working together with our teammates and coaches to improve our skills are good things. But when the energy that motivates our competition is oriented toward destroying or demoralizing our opponents, we're not living as we were created to live. Competitive engagement with others requires that we think wisely about how we will behave toward an opponent *before* and *after* a vigorous game. While greeting opponents, athletes can move beyond a feigned kindness by offering a warm handshake or a word of encouragement. Consider what it means to represent God even while playing hard against an opponent. As we show true respect and leave behind our envy or sense of superiority and pride, we leave a far more lasting impression than do the numbers on the scoreboard.[8]

A PRAYER TO CARE

Everywhere you go, your mind and body go with you. I know, pretty profound, isn't it? Making a difference from our own corner of the world begins as we learn to care for the life we've been given. You have only one body. So take time to care for yourself, physically and emotionally. This will directly affect the impact you can make in the world.

We need professionals and volunteers who willingly give of their time and skills to care for people. The proper care and treatment of God's image bearers is one of the most significant ways we can make a difference in the world. Together we offer up this simple prayer: "Sanctify, O Lord, those whom you have called to the study and practice of the arts of healing, and to the prevention of disease and pain. Strengthen them by your life-giving Spirit that by their ministries the health of the community may be promoted and your creation glorified; through Jesus Christ our Lord. Amen."[9]

BEFORE YOU TURN THE PAGE

Reflect

1. How does this view of health care compare with how you've previously thought about health care?
2. What's the most challenging part of approaching health and wellness this way?
3. Which story or example connects with you most? Why?
4. As an individual or as a health care professional, how can you begin applying these ideas?

Act

1. Outline a plan for your self-care. What priorities do you need to make for the next six months?
2. If you're a health-care professional, look at today's schedule and pray for the patients and clients you'll see. Even two minutes spent doing this can change your orientation for the day.
3. Pay attention to what's behind the symptoms you observe—for the benefit of both the individual and others.
4. Determine how and where you can give your "4 percent"—locally and/or globally.
5. Create an atmosphere of optimism and comfort for patients. Consider the music you play in your office, the manner in which people are greeted on the phone, and the resources available for patients and their families.

CHAPTER 8

KIDS' HEROES

TEACHERS, FAMILY, AND FRIENDS

My girls, Emily and Grace, are on the cusp of adolescence. And they're surrounded by voices vying for a piece of their imagination. Everywhere we turn, someone is trying to recruit them to be lifelong customers. Competing against Disney, Nintendo, and Abercrombie & Fitch, Linda and I have to work extra hard to remind our girls that they were made for so much more than boyfriends, stardom, money, and sex appeal. Thankfully, we're not alone in our quest to raise godly young women. We're blessed with a community of friends and family who speak into their lives. And although they've had a few teachers along the way who have implicitly taught them that grades, a good college, and a successful career are the most important things in life, they've had far more who have said to them, "You are your relationships, your values, and your service." I'm so grateful we have such a supportive community of adults helping us shape our girls.

Michelle Day is an elementary school teacher who taught both our girls. Michelle grew up in our town. In middle school, Michelle asked her dad to drop her off a few blocks away from school so people wouldn't see their old car. But Michelle's hardworking parents taught her there's no shame in being who you are. They taught her to care for people near and far. Michelle never imagined she'd be teaching in her own school district ten years later, but if you see her in the classroom, you can immediately tell—she was made to teach! Michelle continually exposes her second-graders to the needs of other students in the classroom, the needs of people living a few blocks away, and the realities faced by people in other parts of the world. Linda and I have always said to our girls, "Wants don't equal *needs*." But hearing Mrs. Day say the same thing during an economics unit caught their attention! Now they're as quick to catch me when I say, "I *need* coffee!"

Michelle doesn't talk down to her second-graders, and she won't allow them to do that with each other. Instead she treats them with respect. I'll never forget my confusion when Grace came home one day beaming as she told me Mrs. Day asked her to redo part of the report she turned in. In one section of the report, Grace was supposed to compare herself with the doctor she had just read about, and she wrote, "Dr. Elizabeth Blackwell was really smart. I'm not." Michelle wrote in big letters on the paper, "You're not allowed to say that, Grace, because you *are* smart. You need to correct this." Don't assume that all this emphasis on positive encouragement means Michelle's class is a breeze and a place where kids rule. She reaches her boiling point when a student treats a peer poorly. She'll pull the student aside and talk with them about their behavior. Emily and Grace were powerfully shaped in Michelle's classroom as she lived out her faith in our public school.

Emily and Grace Livermore

This chapter includes inspiring stories about people building schools for kids in Afghanistan, teaching underprivileged students in the inner city, and adopting orphans. But coaches, teachers, and aunts and uncles who invest in "average" suburban kids are also part of God's redemptive work around the world. We're going to explore different ways to change the world by working with kids—whether they are our own children, our nieces and nephews, our students, or our fellow neighbors all over the globe.

IMAGINATION AND IDENTITY

Shane Claiborne, a Christian activist for the poor, says, "Instead of asking young people, 'What are you going to do when you grow up?' ask them, 'Who are you becoming?' *The question is not whether you will be a doctor or a lawyer but what kind of doctor or lawyer you will be.*"[1] One of the most important roles we play as we work with the kids and students in our lives is giving them an imagination to live the best possible life—a life defined by surrender to Jesus, being an image bearer of God, and joining God's work in the world. Who are the family members, teachers, and youth leaders who will give children a clear picture of how they were created to live?

We live in an age when a few massive corporations control most of the media and entertainment industry. As a result, the message kids often hear comes from a few blaring voices. When watching a movie produced by Universal Pictures, think about the implicit messages coming from their owner, General Electric (GE). Or when hearing a report on *NBC Nightly News* about the greening of nuclear power, remember that NBC's owner, also GE, has more than a passing interest in the development of nuclear power plants![2] Switch the channel to ABC and consider what its owner, Disney, is interested in selling you. Pick up a copy of *Family Fun* at the magazine stand, check out a library book published by Hyperion Press, or listen to music produced by Hollywood Records, and you've only begun to consume from Walt Disney's massive empire.

I'm not trying to vilify groups like Disney and GE. There are people within these multibillion-dollar industries who are living out the kinds of values we've been exploring in earlier chapters. But we're wise to be alert to the sprawling influence of groups like GE, Time Warner, Disney, and Viacom on our kids and us.

Alongside these blaring voices are the quieter but influential words and actions of teachers like Kaelynn Benham, Emily and Grace's fourth-grade teacher. As a teacher, Kaelynn's commitment is to shape the imagination and identity of her students by giving them a healthy self-confidence and showing them that they can make a real difference in the world. She's trying to drown out the barrage of messages coming at kids that tells them something different. Kaelynn has spent time with teachers and students in Zambia as well as in her Michigan classroom. She notes the profound differences between the two contexts, but in both places, she sees the desperate need for students to see themselves as God does. She says, "I see God's hand at work when I witness a student's confidence soar while accomplishing a task, a genuine smile showing a sense of self-worth, a new friendship being made, and other symbols of love and compassion shared from one student to another."

Scot and Monique Bale live in a rural Midwest community with their four kids. They supplement the homeschool curriculum they use with articles, books, and videos about global issues. The Bales make regular trips to visit shut-ins who live nearby, they save money to support a few global organizations and causes, and they pray daily for some overseas friends. Scot and Monique want their kids to know that success isn't defined by money and fame. They have much higher dreams for their kids — to live as God's ambassadors in the world, whether that means staying in their rural community, moving to the city, or working overseas.

THE GIFT OF EDUCATION

Teachers and coaches can organize students to volunteer in the community or raise funds to help people in Africa, but the primary way teachers serve the world is through excellent teaching. We've probably all been inspired by a great teacher. Maybe it was a college professor who made a subject come to life for you, or a fifth-grade teacher who believed in you when no one else did. Perhaps a piano teacher or a coach did more than prepare you for the upcoming competition; they became a confidante and mentor as well. Teachers have the privilege of sharing the excitement of new ideas with students and seeing them grow as they come to discover God's world. The best teachers continue to develop themselves as learners—growing both in their subject area and in specialized knowledge of how to teach well. Incidentally, this happens in adult education as well, so although most of this chapter is directed toward our relationships with kids, some of it is also relevant to those who teach older age groups. Education itself is a redemptive gift. It can awaken hearts and minds to God's world and allows others to live out their priestly function—to join God in making the world a better place.

I recently heard a Christian leader who was excited about his wife's new job as a middle school math teacher. He said, "She doesn't really care about teaching kids algebra, but this is a great doorway for her to share her faith with students and their families." His statement unnerved me. I hope Emily's math teacher cares about teaching her math! Viewing a teaching job in light of the world's needs should mean more than just using the classroom as a front for undercover evangelism! There are many creative ways teachers can interject their faith, but surely it should not come at the expense of good teaching.

In the person of Jesus, we encounter a teacher who was very responsive to the people he taught. Jesus didn't answer every question he was asked; instead he asked probing questions and encouraged people to think wisely. He shared in their burdens and joys, helped to unleash people's gifts and passions, and communicated with imagery, narrative, and concrete examples. Read the Gospels with an eye toward how Jesus taught.

We often think about the "haves and have-nots" in the context of money, but this phrase applies equally well in the context of educational opportunity. Some would even argue that the lack of an education is a far worse form of poverty because ignorance further exacerbates the struggle of those caught in a cycle of oppression and financial poverty. Consider for a moment that 67 percent of the people in the world can't even read! Whether it's grade school, high school, college, or adult education classes, a good education largely sets the trajectory for the rest of an individual's life. More educators are needed who are willing to make the gift of education available to these educational have-nots.

Greg Mortenson, a mountain climber from Montana, stumbled upon the crying need for a good education in his attempt to climb K2, the world's second-highest mountain, in the Karakoram Range of Pakistan. Greg ended up stranded and injured in the village of Korphe, where he met a group of children just sitting in the dirt, writing with sticks in the sand. There was no school in the village, because a teacher would cost a dollar a day, more than this simple village could afford. Instead the village shared a teacher with a neighboring village, holding classes three days a week. On the other days, the kids practiced their lessons in the dirt. There were no pencils or paper or other supplies for the children. Having been nurtured back to strength by the Korphe people, Mortenson promised them he would return someday and build a school. Out of that rash promise came a harrowing journey as Mortenson reoriented his life to fulfill his commitment. To date, he's established over ninety schools in rural and often volatile regions of Pakistan and Afghanistan, schools which provide the gift of education to over thirty-four thousand children, including twenty-four thousand girls, for whom few educational opportunities existed previously. One Pakistani army general, Bashir Baz, told Mortenson, "The only way to defeat [terrorism] is to build relationships with these people, to draw them into the modern world with education and business. Otherwise, the fight will go on forever."[3] Mortenson is fighting the war on terror, one school at a time. TV newscaster Tom Brokaw describes Mortenson's story as "proof that one ordinary person, with the right combination of character and determination, really can change the world."[4] While most of us won't end up building a hundred schools overseas, don't discount the powerful role education plays in God's redemption.

Even in North America, many people lack access to a good education. In the United States, this is particularly true for those who live in economically challenged neighborhoods where public schools have limited teachers, textbooks, and other essential resources.

In the late seventies, John Booy had a Mortenson-like experience in Midwest U.S.A. John was a long-haired radical who had just moved into one of the poorest neighborhoods in Grand Rapids, Michigan. He looked around and saw kids who were dealing with crushing problems—fistfights at home, parents who couldn't pay rent, moms and dads on drugs or in jail, and regular gang problems. Going to school, if they even got there in the first place, didn't seem to help much. Teachers were short on patience and were expected to manage huge classrooms with few resources, gang activity filled the hallways, and put-downs and negative peer pressure were everywhere.

John recruited some of his friends, and they started teaching twelve students in a church basement, forming a small school they called Potter's House. Now, almost thirty years later, John continues to live in the same neighborhood and continues to lead the Potter's House school. Today the school has more than five hundred students from prekindergarten through twelfth grade, representing twenty-five countries. Last year, the school had a 100 percent graduation rate. And there's a waiting list to get in. A large amount of John's time is spent fund-raising for the school so they can offer affordable tuition based on a student's family income. But the students are what keep him involved. John knows the name of every student, and he greets each of them as they enter school every morning. From the minute they come into the building, these children are known and loved. Many of them have been through difficult and challenging life experiences: refugee camps, parents working two or three jobs, and people regularly moving in and out of their house. John says, "We want this to be their oasis. This is their family." John believes you *can* change the world—one student at a time. "The kids are just waiting," he says.

Camps are another place where the gift of education can be powerfully passed on to children. Nicole, a college student who has spent several summers counseling at a camp for foster kids, had her cabin of girls throw a surprise birthday party for one of the campers, a young girl named Shontaya. Shontaya was the life of the cabin all week long, but when her cabinmates threw her the surprise party at the end of the week, Nicole was shocked to see Shontaya suddenly appear withdrawn and sad. Shontaya stared at the ground as her cabinmates sang "Happy Birthday," and she barely acknowledged the party. Later Shontaya told Nicole she thought the whole thing had to be a joke on her because she had never had a birthday cake or a party before. She didn't think she deserved it.

Education empowers people to think for themselves and to take initiative to change their circumstances. Tyrannical rulers know this. As noted earlier, university campuses are the first places to be shut down in the midst of social unrest. The idealism of young students combined with the atmosphere of open inquiry make campuses and schools bastions for alternative ways of seeing the world. Good education helps people embrace their image-bearing capacity to think for themselves and act on their convictions and ideas.[5]

THE POWER OF A CHILD

Barbara Vogel believes in the potential of children because of what she's seen them accomplish. Vogel is a fifth-grade teacher in Aurora, Colorado, and often looks for ways to help her students understand global realities. A few years ago she read to her class an article about slavery in Sudan, and the students were motivated to take action. They decided to buy back some of the slaves and began raising money by selling lemonade, T-shirts, and used toys. They wrote a letter to the editor of the local newspaper, and it eventually grabbed the attention of *CBS Evening News*, which in turn led to donations of fifty thousand dollars. They also began an awareness campaign, writing letters to national and international leaders and urging them to end slavery in Sudan. Hundreds of Sudanese were freed as a result of Vogel and her students' work. Vogel said, "My goal is to show the power of children, to show that children want to help, and to show adults what children can do."[6]

Many other kids have gotten involved in the Sudan crisis as well. Larissa started raising money to help Darfur refugees when she was ten. She says, "You have to stand up for what is right and fight for what you believe in. No matter how young or old you are, you can make a difference if you put your heart into it."[7] For several years,

Larissa has used as many school assignments as possible to learn and share more about the Sudan crisis. She sold her massive Barbie collection, and she organizes garage sales to raise additional funds. Her imagination was captured by something that matters.

Emily was ten years old when she decided to do something about the HIV/AIDS crisis in Rwanda. Her dad, Don Golden, frequently travels to East Africa as part of his work with World Relief, and he includes his family in his work by telling them about some of the situations people face there. Emily was gripped by what HIV/AIDS was doing to her peers in Rwanda, and she started a project called Kids for Compassion (*www.freewebs.com/kidsforcompassion*). She and her friend Kelli started raising money to help send Rwandan kids affected by HIV/AIDS to school. They raise funds by collecting pop cans, by asking people to organize and hold fund-raisers, and by requesting donations. Kids for Compassion provides funding for school fees, transportation, school supplies, and some medical or individual needs that may arise. Ten-year-olds helping ten-year-olds. It's a beautiful thing.

My own daughter Emily is a huge animal lover, and she's recruited her sister Grace into her causes. There's always some kind of advocacy effort for animals going on in our house. Whether they're walking dogs to earn donations for the Humane Society, making posters about puppy mills, or rescuing ducklings separated from their mothers, Emily and Grace extend God's care to a lot of animals.

It can be daunting to help kids grapple with horrible problems such as slavery, HIV/AIDS, or genocide. But educating kids and allowing them to be part of the solution gives them a chance to live out their God-given role. Kids are very impressionable, and we have to deal with that reality in responsible ways. But as the creative power of children is unleashed, we will see more of God's shalom throughout the world, for generations to come.

STEWARDING A PRECIOUS GIFT

Few things better reveal someone's character than the way they treat children. And the real test is the way a person treats a child when no one else is watching. It's one thing for me to talk with my friends' kids or with the children of people I'm trying to impress. As a parent, I know how endearing it is to watch people pay attention to my girls. But how do I treat the kid who walks by me on the street? What kind of respect do I give a child when their parents aren't around?

Many of the examples we've encountered have been teachers and educational leaders. But the ideas we've explored in this chapter apply to parents, grandparents, youth leaders, coaches, camp counselors, and anyone who has the privilege of working with or interacting with kids—all of us! We can all shape the lives of children by helping them see what really matters in life.

June 5, 1999, was one of the best days of my life, and one of the worst days of my life. My daughter Grace was born that day. Filled with the joy of a father when I held her in my arms, I felt like I could conquer the world. A few hours later, though, I received an unexpected phone call from my mother, who told me that my dad had just died. In one chaotic day, I experienced the full circle of life. I am a product both of my parents' godly influence and of their relentless commitment to nurture me to be who God intended me to be. And I'm trying to pass on what they have given to me, by investing in the lives of Emily and Grace. Each year, on Grace's birthday, I'm reminded of my responsibility to steward the precious lives given to me as I reflect on my own father and his godly imprint on my life. Children are the most precious resource we possess in this world. Making a difference in the world doesn't require that you travel far from home. It's as close as the nearest child.

BEFORE YOU TURN THE PAGE

Reflect

1. What teachers or parental figures have been role models for you? What makes them different from others?
2. What's the most challenging part of helping kids live the way God intended them to live?
3. Which story or example connects with you most? Why?

4. How can you begin applying these ideas with kids in your life?

Act

1. Assign students to research and report on a variety of global crises.
2. Make books and videos available that describe global issues in age-appropriate ways.
3. Interject international examples when teaching basic values like diversity, respect, and happiness.
4. Empower kids to organize a community-wide initiative to respond to an issue they care about.
5. Help kids develop relationships with people from other parts of the world — refugees, foreign students, immigrants, and so on.

CHAPTER 9

CAUTION

SIGNPOSTS FOR THE JOURNEY AHEAD

I hope the stories and ideas from these varied fields inspire you as much as they have me. There are unprecedented opportunities to make a global difference right where you are, without ever leaving home or changing careers. In the final section of the book, you'll find a series of exercises to help you discern how you can get started. But first, a story and a few words of caution.

A suburban church in the Chicago area runs an annual Christmas program where dads and sons spend a December Saturday in an inner-city neighborhood distributing gifts to underresourced kids there. One year, they decided to partner with Jamar's church on the south side of the city. Jamar was grateful for their generous spirit, but he asked the suburban men to help him set up a temporary store at his church instead. This would be a place where they could sell the donated gifts at seriously reduced prices to the neighborhood parents. As a result, the parents in the neighborhood would have the honor of buying gifts for their own kids. The suburban church said no. Having their dads and sons personally deliver the gifts was too important to them. This part of the program was what made the experience such an annual highlight for them. Jamar was disappointed, but he later said to me, "The last thing I need is one more message to kids in our neighborhood that says, *Guess what. This six-year-old white kid got you a better gift than your schmuck of a father did.*"[1]

Stories like this should make us stop and ask, What's the motivation behind our desire to make a difference in the world? Many of us start out with good intentions, but if we aren't careful, our good intentions easily get mixed up with self-serving motives and can sometimes end up having the *opposite* effect of what we intended. To avoid this, there are a few signposts to direct how we get involved.

SIGNPOST 1: LISTEN TO THE LOCALS

The answer for the men in the suburban church wasn't to leave well enough alone at Jamar's church but to trust the local expertise and insight of a leader like Jamar. The best hope for the south side of Chicago lies in the south side of Chicago. The same is true for China, Mozambique, and Lebanon. It's not that we as outsiders have nothing to offer. But our service should always involve listening to and partnering with the local residents.

In particular, we should ask how we can join what the local Christians are doing to address a need. Every country in the world has some presence of a Christian church, either gathered or scattered. So we should always look for ways to partner with what's already happening somewhere rather than blowing in as the great Western saviors. This should be our default approach, whether we're serving in the next county or twelve time zones away.

Every church and community has resources, and every church and community has needs. There's no question most Westerners have resources that can meet the needs of people in places like Rwanda and Afghanistan. But Rwandans and Afghans have resources too. How can we develop reciprocal relationships with people in other parts of the world? Adopt the posture of a listener and a learner.

SIGNPOST 2: EVALUATE

Sometimes *measurement* and *assessment* get treated as four-letter words when it comes to charitable efforts. *How can you quantify*

God's transformation?! Only God knows the effectiveness and the eternal fruit of our efforts! How would Jesus have measured up against a metric? I agree we need to be careful when it comes to assessing the work of ministry, but this doesn't mean we should ignore evaluating the effectiveness of our work.

Furthermore, the intended beneficiaries must be involved in the evaluation and assessment process. Economist William Easterly asks, "Why not give the poor voices on whether aid is reaching them?"[2] If a cause is worthy of our resources and effort, it's worthy of us being willing to ask tough questions. Is this really the best way to respond to the issue? What can we learn from others who have been working on this? What do individuals closest to the issue have to say about it? Take time to do the hard work of assessing your efforts and the efforts of those with whom you partner. If the suburban church had started by asking Jamar how to best help, an entirely different approach could have emerged.

SIGNPOST 3: BEWARE OF GRAND PANACEAS

While I hope I have inspired you to make a difference in the world, we need to be careful with this whole idea of being a "world changer." Andy Crouch suggests we need to hold our activism in tension with the reality that *only God ultimately changes the world.* If we're honest, we'll admit we have a hard enough time changing our own little lives—keeping our promises, breaking free of our addictions and habits, and releasing our grudges. Crouch writes, "We have changed less about ourselves than we would like to admit. Who are we to charge off and change the world?"[3] World changing is something God does. But God still invites us to join him along the way to do *our* part.

The longer you study the global realities and problems facing our generation, the more you begin to grasp their complexity. For example, are sweatshops a cause of poverty or a symptom of it? While it's easy to demonize sweatshop owners who offer low wages and miserable working conditions, some people have suggested that banning sweatshops might make poverty worse. Neuo, a Cambodian girl who spends her days scavenging the dump for plastic says, "I'd love to get a job in a factory.... At least it's in the shade."[4] Writing about her, *New York Times* columnist Nicholas Kristof asserts, "The best way to help people in the poorest countries isn't to campaign against sweatshops but to promote manufacturing there.... Look, I know that Americans have a hard time accepting that sweatshops can help people. But take it from thirteen-year-old Neuo Chantout, who earns a bit less than one dollar a day scavenging in the dump.... She worries about her sister, who lost part of her hand when a garbage truck ran over her. 'It's dirty, hot and smelly here,' she said. 'A factory is better.'"[5]

I'm unsettled by Kristof's point, but I can't entirely dismiss it either! There are no grand panaceas or simple solutions for eradicating poverty or terrorism. But don't let the complexities discourage you either. Replace your visionary ambitions for universal solutions with homegrown, grassroots, piecemeal changes, and take one step at a time.

SIGNPOST 4: LEARN FROM EXPERTS

Whatever your field, continue to grow and learn. Your expertise and ongoing development as a musician, business leader, or innovative teacher is directly connected to your role in global mission. The greatest needs of the world require more than enthusiasm and zeal. The problems we face today need people with strong expertise and experience combined with a learner's attitude. College students, don't look at your studies as a waste of time. If you have the chance to read, discern, and reflect on a specific field for a season, it can be a valuable part of your lifelong global service. Don't limit the possibilities God may have in your future, and don't miss the ways you can serve where you are right now. Your campus has needs. The papers you research and write can address global issues and inspire change in your life and in the lives of your friends and teachers.

Our North American ethos tends to elevate passion and zeal over knowledge and expertise. But we need to reclaim an appropriate respect for individuals who devote their attention and work to specific topics and skills. If I suddenly learned that a family member had a fatal disease, I'd do more than pray and get a bunch of friends to visit. I'd look for the best experts I could find to help. Sometimes we treat poverty, killer diseases, and human trafficking as if money, prayer, and short-term missions trips are all we need to fix these problems. But there are organizations and experts who have invested loads of time, money, study, and life experience into learning about these issues and their causes. As we connect our work and interest with the expertise of others, there can be a far greater return from our global efforts. Commit to your own ongoing learning, and work with others who have expertise in the global issues you're concerned about.

SIGNPOST 5: IMPROVE YOUR CQ

Finally, our efforts are more likely to meet the groans of the world when combined with cultural intelligence. Cultural intelligence (CQ) is the capability to function effectively across a variety of cultures.[6] It's a skill set anyone can develop. The goal isn't to become like whomever we're with, and we don't have to become an expert on every culture. But the emphasis of CQ is to understand and respect the differences between us and those of other cultures so we can more effectively work and serve together. Based on research across thirty countries, cultural intelligence can be understood as a four-step process that can be used when facing any cross-cultural assignment:

Step 1, CQ Drive: What's my motivation for this cross-cultural assignment?
Step 2, CQ Knowledge: What cultural understanding do I need to do this effectively?
Step 3, CQ Strategy: What's my plan?
Step 4, CQ Action: What behaviors should I adopt to do this respectfully and effectively?[7]

Cultural intelligence offers you an overall repertoire of understanding and skills for working with people and issues in a variety of contexts. I've written extensively on cultural intelligence elsewhere. Visit *www.CulturalQ.com* for more information, including ways to assess and develop your CQ.

ABOVE ALL ELSE, LOVE

Recently a Chinese pastor shared with me his frustration with Bible smugglers from the West. He's seen countless short-term missions teams "bomb" his town during the night by stuffing tracts and Bibles into people's bicycle baskets and mailboxes. They claimed that when people awoke the next morning, "Jesus was everywhere." This pastor wasn't so sure. He wonders if these undercover agents are more interested in a James Bond adventure for Jesus than in slowing down to find out what Jesus looks like through the local believers who are faithfully living out the presence of Jesus in this town year after year.

Despite alarming stories like this one, there are all kinds of Christians who are making a difference in a much better way. Rather than being paralyzed by the critiques of people like this pastor or Jamar, the pastor from the south side of Chicago, some individuals are heeding these critiques and using them to improve the way they get involved all over the world.

Adventure, feeling good about ourselves, shame, guilt, and a need for control are some of the underlying agendas that often mix with more noble intentions for missional service. But as we continually subdue our self-serving agendas by striving to love above all else, we can reflect God's redeeming efforts in beautiful ways. *Do* get involved. But do so with these cautions in mind as you seek to discern how you can uniquely make the contribution God has invited you to make.

BEFORE YOU TURN THE PAGE

One of the best things you can do to reflect and act on the material in this chapter is to continue your learning on these issues. Consider reading one of the following books to take you farther in navigating the potholes on the road ahead:

Cultural Intelligence: Improving Your CQ to Engage Our Multicultural World by David Livermore

Culture Making: Recovering Our Creative Calling by Andy Crouch

Not on Our Watch by Don Cheadle and John Prendergast
Saving the World at Work by Tim Sanders
Serving with Eyes Wide Open: Doing Short-Term Missions with Cultural Intelligence by David Livermore
When Helping Hurts: How to Alleviate Poverty without Hurting the Poor by Brian Fikkert and Steve Corbett

PART 3

YOUR NEXT STEP

Now it's your turn. Yes, you. You've read the stories of others, so where should *you* get involved? What issue matters to you? How do you make this practical and actually do something? This final section is written to help you take the next step in making our world a better place.

Many people want to get more involved globally, but they decide they have to delay their participation for several years. The priorities of paying off school debt, getting established in a career, and raising a family take precedence. Many use an occasional short-term missions trip or a financial donation to pacify the innate longing to do more. Some hope to retire early so they can do more of this kind of thing. But why relegate the essence of our humanity to an occasional trip and to the delayed gratification of doing more in twenty years? And as our lives fill with other priorities, will it ever actually happen?

This final part of the book is more like a guidebook. So grab a pen and a journal and jot down your insights and thoughts. You're the expert here. How can you intentionally shape your time, work, relationships, and money toward living as God's partner in the world?

The questions and exercises in chapter 10 can help you discern your part in all this personally. Chapter 11 is intended for use by a group of people wanting to serve together — your family, your church, or another group.

CHAPTER 10

YOUR JOURNEY

DISCERNING YOUR CONTRIBUTION

We can't say yes to every need. So how do we align our lives with the great causes of our day? What's *your* part in global mission? This is where we began our conversation. There are far too many needs in the world for us to tackle all of them. How do you justify supporting schools in Afghanistan when many U.S. schools are in disarray? Why help homeless children in L.A. when there are far more in Mumbai? How can you make a career of saving the whales when there are millions who have yet to hear about Jesus? How does volunteer research on coral destruction address the global atrocities on tonight's news?

I decided I wanted to be a missionary when I was eleven years old. It was during our church's annual missions conference, complete with cool snakeskin displays, colorful flags, and the ubiquitous "international" potluck. On the last night of the conference, I walked the aisle and declared that I was going to be a missionary. I spent the next few days mapping out the next twenty years of my life, including when I'd arrive in Brazil (which just so happened to be where the conference speaker was a missionary). I was an intense kid. I began telling people my twenty-year plan. My dad, in his wisdom, affirmed my interest in serving as a missionary but suggested I might want to temper my bold statements about what the next twenty years were going to look like. *He has no clue!* I thought. *I've heard from God on this!*

The next summer, I heard a speaker at camp who was a missionary in Alaska. Suddenly I thought that sounded like a cool place I should consider. And the following October, our missions conference was filled with missionaries from various countries in Africa. Now there were even more options on the table, and I began to wonder if my dad was on to something.

Thirty years later, my life has evolved pretty differently from my plans as an eleven-year-old. My journey has been a convergence of my choices and efforts combined with God's divine providence. I don't understand how that all works together, but I'm drawn into the mystery of it all. My only regret is that I've spent so much of my life worrying about whether I'd find ways to connect my interests, gifts, and longings with the world's deepest needs. In retrospect, God has faithfully continued to weave these things together in ways that far surpass my plans—at eleven or forty!

The question of where and how we should get involved in the global scene can be overwhelming for most people. Whose need is greatest? Which country, which war, and what issue should I tackle? How do my skills, interests, and life circumstances connect with these needs? These kinds of questions can be paralyzing. But remember: God won't waste your desire to make a difference in the world. Sometimes I've had to reel in my global ambitions to tend to urgent needs in my own family or my work. But in hindsight, even those seasons have been opportunities to connect with God's work all over the world, even if I couldn't see it at the time. Throughout this chapter, we'll look at several core issues involved with discerning our part in God's global work, and you'll have a chance to take a personal inventory to help you see where you fit into the work God is doing.

OUR FIRST CALLING

Say the word *calling*, as in "What's your calling?" and those of us in the Western world immediately conjure up images of writing personal mission statements, discerning our SHAPE,[1] and tackling issues great and small in the world. But for Christians, our calling begins with *who we are in Christ*. The Scriptures have far more to say about calling as it relates to our relationship with Christ than they do about calling in the sense of what we're supposed to "do" for God. *The primary idea of calling in the Bible is to an integrated life of faith and devotion to God.* Our identity lies in having been called by Christ, to Christ, and for Christ. Christian scholar Os Guinness writes, "First and foremost, we are called to Some*one* (God), not to some*thing* (such as motherhood, politics, or teaching) or to some*where* (such as the inner city or Outer Mongolia)."[2] Calling is a matter of moving from who we are today to who God calls us to become.

When you combine my global interests with my type A personality, it's really easy for me to lose sight of my primary calling in Christ. I'm always striving to make more impact in more places with more people in more ways. Sometimes my striving to accomplish more and more for Jesus comes from a skewed understanding of my primary identity in Christ. I've spent too many years of my life trying to impress others so they will take notice of the great things I'm doing for God.

Throughout this book, I've been highlighting our identity as cocreators with God. God invites us to work together with him to make the world a better place. But our work with God isn't the only dimension to our identity. To get at this, let's look at the apostle Paul's letter to his friends in Ephesus. Keep in mind that the Christian Ephesians were being pummeled by persecution as they received this letter. I would've expected Paul to start his letter with a pep talk about hanging in there despite the beatings and abuse. But he doesn't do that. He bursts in with a rich description of who they are in Christ. At first blush, Paul's words feel a bit obtuse. But the longer I look at his words, the more compelling I find Paul's approach. These persecuted Christians needed a reminder of their true identity more than anything else. First and foremost, Paul reminds them that they aren't *primarily* the persecuted, oppressed citizens of Ephesus. In effect, Paul writes, "Look ... You're among the people of God! God has lavished you with mercy and kindness and has let you in on his secret plan." Spend a few minutes reading Ephesians 1 and note the generous language used to describe their identity.

Who Am I?

Read Ephesians 1.

Write down all the descriptions of who we are as the adopted children of God (there's the first one for your list!).

This is who you are—your *calling.* This is the core of your identity. Go on to read Ephesians 2, and the rich descriptions continue. You're made alive in Christ, saved, raised up with Christ, God's workmanship, created to do good works, brought near, and the list keeps going and going and going. Notice, though, that not one of these descriptions is tied to anything we do. These are unconditional descriptions of who we are as the children of God.

Our identity must precede our activity. If I know who I am, I know what I'm going to do. There's a seamless connection between our lifelong devotion to Jesus and living, speaking, and acting on his behalf. One without the other is incomplete. Therefore, although it's appropriate to say we've been "called" to practice law or go into business or provide clean water filters to Bangladesh, these callings are an outgrowth of our primary calling in life—to live in ever-growing relationship with Christ.[3]

Here's my point: No job, career, or cause is big enough to shape our eternal identity. Putting our whole selves into our work or into meeting the needs of the world will sabotage us. We need a deeper sense of calling that includes the call to deeper intimacy with Jesus—an identity that will last forever.

THE WORLD NEEDS EVERYTHING; JUST DO SOMETHING!

Needs and problems exist all around us, so where do we begin? The realities we explored in chapter 1 can leave us overwhelmed and paralyzed. Why should we choose *this* issue and not *that* one? What can I possibly do about the alarming numbers of kids trafficked in the world for sex and war? And what's the *biggest* need? Who decides?

The truth is, the world needs everything! Name an issue, and there's probably a way you can be involved in it. So pick something, and you can't go wrong. You *can't* solve everything. But you *can* do something. Don't start playing the comparison game of evaluating how much more impact somebody else is making with the issue they're involved in. On the other hand, don't be the one who acts as if "my cause can beat up your cause."

You've been called to be the presence of Jesus with someone, somewhere. You can't fully determine the results. Those are up to God. But you can faithfully live out your calling as God's partner in the world. That child you mentor could end up being the next Mother Teresa ... or she might be another deadbeat mom. The one tree you save as a biologist in Bolivia could help researchers find the cancer cure that saves millions ... or it might "simply" prevent erosion in a local village. Some people might spend their time organizing a reading group that causes suburbanites to rethink how they spend their money ... and others might develop a microfinance program for a tribal group in Southeast Asia. Some people might compose works of music that bring joy to a global audience ... while others might bring a smile to children in a classroom by writing a poem about them.

Some will take on large-scale causes. Others will mentor one child at a time. Some will get to see big results, and others might see a few small changes, but changes that make a lasting difference. There are no qualitative or quantitative comparisons that really make sense when evaluating the importance of particular issues. The downstream effects of our efforts are largely unknown.[4] When you find the cause, issue, or people group that interests you, pour yourself into it and make no apologies. You can't be equally engaged in every issue. But you can be confident that when you extend God's reach to an issue near to your heart and giftings, God will use it to redeem the world.

There's no single formula for discovering your role in the world. We'll have friends who describe a Damascus Road–like epiphany that results in a sudden awareness of their calling. These kinds of encounters are usually powerful for the individuals who have them. They might experience a calling like this through a major event, or it might come as they are taking a quiet walk in the woods, reading a book, or going about their daily business. For those who have these types of awakening moments, great! But those of us without experiences like this need not feel as though we've been given a second-class calling.

Others discover calling amid a major life change, something they may or may not have chosen. Births, deaths, marriage, divorce, a sudden illness, a sudden job change can all be the kinds of things that suddenly alter your view of life and elicit a new sense of calling. Some of the best advocates for Downs Syndrome research are parents and siblings of kids with Downs. Many of the best activists against drug trafficking are former drug addicts. New parents might learn they are passionate about teaching or nurturing others. Life tends to bring us unexpected circumstances that often shape the way we think about our calling.

For most of us, discerning our calling will be an ongoing journey of discovery. Through intuition, experiences, reflection, and the input of others, we'll move in and out of lots of different ways to serve. Some might spend forty years serving a particular cause, while others might serve fourteen different causes over a decade. Be free from thinking that your pursuits need to mirror the experiences of others. Let's learn all we can from one another and celebrate the diversity of our callings — both the causes to which we're called and the ways we discover and pursue our callings.[5]

PERSONAL DISCOVERY

So is there anything we can *do* to help us discover what to do, where, and with whom? Personal discovery requires a high degree of self-awareness, something often absent from our frenzied world. The whole idea of stepping back to better understand ourselves just runs so counterintuitive to our constantly moving, frenetic culture. Many of us get so busy juggling our day-to-day responsibilities that we become strangers to ourselves. When asked to truly describe who we are, what we care about, and what matters most to us, we might find ourselves reluctant to respond. The absence of the time and space to reflect wears on our ability to dream and imagine, and it deafens us to the voice within.

It's pretty difficult to know how to respond to the world's needs if we don't adequately know ourselves. What makes your heart sing? Where do you find your greatest enjoyment? What motivates you? What drains you? What are the causes that most inspire you? What atrocities most incite you? We'll get to questions like these in a minute. But the process begins by becoming more personally aware.

Parker Palmer, a highly respected educator and author, offers some of the most helpful material on the importance of self-awareness for living out our part in God's story. He describes the angst he feels when he observes students taking copious notes on his lectures and PowerPoint slides without a single note written about what's going on within themselves. Most of us aren't accustomed to understanding who we are and who we're becoming. "We listen for guidance everywhere except from within," writes Palmer.[6] As we grow in a fuller understanding of who we were uniquely made to be, we'll find both joy and a pathway to authentic service to others. Palmer writes, "True vocation joins self and service, as Frederick Buechner asserts when he defines vocation as 'the place where your deep gladness meets the world's deep need.' "[7]

Orienting our lives to meet the world's needs begins with understanding ourselves. Here are a few suggestions to increase your personal awareness:

1. Listen

One of the biggest roadblocks to personal discovery is not having the space and posture to slow down and listen. Listening requires a very intentional effort to slow down the RPMs. Although we've never had more time-saving devices at our fingertips, we're busier than ever. Meeting the world's needs begins with listening to and caring for ourselves. The world isn't something that just exists "out there." It's made up of people like us. We begin changing the world by cleaning up our own corner of it, starting with ourselves!

Create the space to listen. Listen to your heart, listen to the Scriptures, and listen to the voices of your community. Sit down, breathe deep, and try to relax. There are a few ways to help us slow down and listen.

For example, silent retreats are growing in popularity. Typically, these are personal retreats where participants give up all media and speaking. Sometimes they're done together with other people, but verbal interaction is restricted to a few brief segments. You might benefit from an organized silent retreat or from just creating your own by grabbing a tent and heading to the woods for a couple days.

If you don't have the luxury of getting away, create a mini-retreat with a quiet walk outside or an evening in front of the fire. These practices can do wonders to put us in a posture to listen. Or try shutting off the music and cell phone in the car and use the mundane task of driving to slow down and listen.

I'm an obsessive journaler. Journaling isn't for everyone. I get that. But for me, getting thoughts from my head down on paper can be a huge way of listening to my soul. I spend so much time on the computer that I need to journal with pen and paper. It slows me down and enhances my ability to listen. Going back to read these reflections can be equally enlightening. And meditate. Get quiet, focus on Scripture with your mind and your heart, and listen.

As you put yourself in a posture of listening, move through these three important exercises:

• • • • • Posturing Ourselves to Listen • • • • •

1. **Confess:** Before rushing off to serve someone or something, what do you need to make right? With whom? With the psalmist, confess your rebellion and desperate need for help: "My sins have overtaken me, and I cannot see. They are more than the hairs of my head, and my heart fails within me. Be pleased to save me, LORD; come quickly, LORD, to help me" (Ps. 40:12–13).

2. **Repent:** Then move from confession to repentance. Affirm to God your desire to live the best possible life, in accordance with how you were intended to live in the world. You were made to reflect the glory and wonder of God and to advance and develop creation.
3. **Surrender:** Submit to God's sovereign rule over your life. Meditate on these ancient words: "Here I am.... I have come to do your will, my God" (Heb. 10:7; see also vv. 5–6 and Ps. 40:6–8).

Write or say this phrase several times: "Here I am.... I have come to do your will, my God." Stop on each word and meditate on it.

Don't rush through this. Whether you have thirty minutes alone at home or a full weekend away, take time to center yourself by putting yourself in a posture to listen.

2. Look Back

Whether you are twenty-two or seventy-five, looking back can be an illuminating part of the discovery process. Some of what was stirring in me when I decided to be a missionary at age eleven may have been little more than my response to the revivalist fervor in my church that night. But I'm convinced some of it was also tied to a stirring in my heart to be involved in what God was doing globally. I didn't grow up globe-trotting, though we regularly traveled from our home in New York to visit my grandparents and extended family in Canada. Even as a child, I was intrigued by some of the subtle differences in food, money, and language on the other side of the border. Then I went on my first short-term missions trip in college and found myself continually wandering from my fellow Americans to seek out the locals. I love interacting with people from different parts of the world. And even though I've since had the chance to work in more than seventy-five countries, I still get an adrenaline rush when I jump on a flight to a new place. Wherever I go, I love to blaze the streets, savor the local food, roam the neighborhoods, and shop at the local markets.

Some of these insights are things I've observed by taking the time to look back over my life. I've had a variety of jobs and interests, but connecting with people and issues from other parts of the world has been a *recurring* interest. Our past doesn't have to define our future, but it certainly offers a window into who we are and who we're becoming.

Birth to Present

Complete a timeline of your life from birth to present.

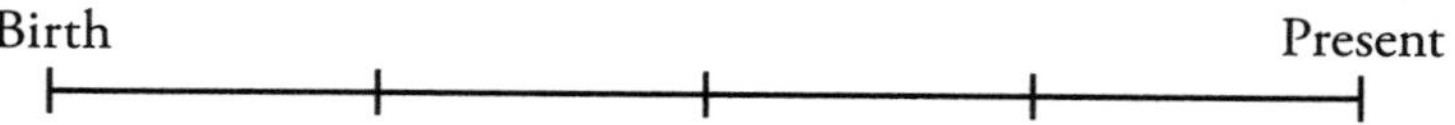

What season of life did you enjoy most? Least?

What markers and events stand out as particularly formative?

What painful memories does this surface?

Remember your childhood and any activities that excited or intrigued you. You may have abandoned them only because you thought doing so was practical at the time, not because you lost your passion for them. What expectations have you had of yourself at different times? What about others' expectations? Make note of as much of this as possible on your timeline. We'll revisit these observations later. Pay attention to the thoughts and feelings that emerge as you spend time looking backward. These can be powerful indicators of things that should impact how you discern your role in partnering with God all over the world.

3. Look Forward

Looking forward can mean anticipating something as soon as next month or as far ahead as the next several decades. What's going on for you right now? What are you looking forward to day to day? What aspect of your work and activities are you enjoying? What are you dreading?

To keep this in perspective, read and reflect on the following passage of Scripture: "Now listen, you who say, 'Today or tomorrow we will go to this or that city, spend a year there, carry on business and make money.' Why, you do not even know what will happen tomorrow. What is your life? You are a mist that appears for a little while and then vanishes. Instead, you ought to say, *'If it is the Lord's will, we will live and do this or that'*" (James 4:13–15, emphasis added).

Repeat the words "Here I am.... I have come to do your will, my God" (Heb. 10:7). Anticipating what's next is healthy as long as we keep these ancient words in perspective. Consider the following:

Looking Forward

What are you looking forward to most right now?

What are you dreading most?

What do you anticipate on the horizon in the next twelve months? Events like graduation, having a baby, retirement, and starting a new business are all changes that should shape our discovery of calling.

What changes do you anticipate in the next five years?

What do you long to be different for you in ten years? What do you hope will be the same?

And what do you want to be when you grow up? It's a question we are often asked as kids. We have fun imagining being our favorite action heroes or living out some other audacious dream. But often, as the reality of life, responsibility, and our limitations sets in, we look back and roll our eyes at our youthful idealism. Can you even answer that question anymore? *What do you want to be when you grow up?*

If given the chance to live out your dream, do you even know what that dream is? What really excites you? If you could be anything, if there were no limitations or obstacles, how would you spend your time? Enhanced self-awareness offers a clearer picture of where our passion lies.

Finally, look all the way forward to the end of your life. Lest this sound really morbid, keep in mind that looking ahead this way demonstrates what's truly important to you. Many of us long to hear Christ say, "Well done, good and faithful servant!" when we complete our time on earth. But what would "good and faithful" look like for your life?

Funeral Planning

What do you hope will be said at your funeral? (As the people close to you remember your life, what do you want to be said? What kind of family member would you like to have been? Friend? Colleague? Church member? Neighbor? World citizen?)

What contributions and achievements do you want the people closest to you to remember?

What difference would you like to have made in the lives of the people left behind?

By slowing down to listen, look back, and look forward, we begin to develop our ability to discern when, how, and where to get involved locally and globally. This posture of personal awareness prepares us to go deeper in examining how to personally engage.

PERSONAL INVENTORY

Next we want to work through some specific questions to guide us in discerning our best contribution to the world. Some of us will benefit by taking the time to work through this inventory at one setting (such as on a silent retreat or on a Saturday when you have some space to yourself). Others might benefit by walking through this a bit at a time over the next several months. Feel free to take your time to complete it.

Later in the chapter, I'll say more about the importance of community for decision making. But for now, pick up a new journal and begin to chronicle your responses to the following items. Don't worry about answering every question, and if the exercises start you thinking about an entirely different topic, follow the rabbit trail for a bit.[8]

1. Personality

Let's begin with understanding your personality. What energizes you? What drains you? What's your personality type? From Myers-Briggs, DISC, and the Big Five personality tests to StrengthFinders and the Enneagram, personality assessments are pretty popular nowadays. Each contributes something different to the process of self-discovery. The Big Five personality test is the most rigorously researched approach to analyzing personality traits, and several free assessments are available online. The Enneagram is rooted in an ancient, spiritual tradition and goes beyond simply enhancing your self-understanding, offering a great deal of insight into the redemptive concerns connected with your personality. The way we're wired shouldn't be in conflict with the callings we pursue. Pay attention to your personality.

Take one of these personality tests. Start with the Big Five, the most academically validated approach to analyzing personality available. Complete the test at *http://similarminds.com/big5.html* and answer the following:

• • • • Understanding Our Personality • • • •

How do the results compare with what you know about yourself? Are there any surprises? (Invite friends and family to help you respond to these questions too! See if they agree with what the test results say. Try not to be too defensive or to overly obsess over what you see and hear from this. This is just one snapshot into who you are.)

What energizes you? (What do you do that makes you feel entirely alive? It might be something closely tied to work, like designing a new product or organizing an event. Or it might be running, hanging out with people, or gardening. Don't overthink it. Just write down things that give you energy and life.)

What drains you? (What are the things that suck the life out of you? Again, these might be work related or otherwise. They probably show up in every part of life. What are the things you don't enjoy doing?)

Don't spend too much time overanalyzing these insights. For now, get them down on paper and see what emerges as you complete this inventory.

Take the next week to examine and reflect on your reactions to the things around you, such as television shows, newspapers, conversations, books, and any other stimuli that pique your interest. What collections do you have? Pay attention to the clues in your own home as to what interests you. Chronicle the things that capture your interest as you continue the discernment process.

2. Skills/Expertise

Now think about the jobs you've had, the volunteer work you've done, and subjects in school you've enjoyed, to get a glimpse of your skill set. When have you felt the most productive and eager to do what you were doing? Notice how these categories overlap. Your personality is usually connected to your skill set, which often relates to your experiences. You have skills that can help meet the pressing needs of our global neighbors.

When you work at something where you possess some natural ability, you'll often feel energized despite setbacks and long hours. These skill sets really come to life when connected with the causes you feel strongly about. Consider the following:

Skills Assessment

What are you good at?

What could you be best at?

What are you most proud of having accomplished in your life? Can you repeat this and further develop it for others?

When do people seek out your advice and counsel? Are there any common themes?

For what would you most like to be acknowledged so far in your life? Don't get all pious and say you don't want any recognition. Of course this is only for the glory of God. But of all the things for which you could be recognized, small or big, for what would recognition be most meaningful to you? This can clue you in on the things that matter most to you.

3. Causes

Now let's think about the causes and issues most important to you. What really sets you off and gets your blood boiling? I'm not talking about pet peeves like slow drivers and telemarketers. I mean the injustices and evils that really get under your skin. This is a powerful indicator of the causes most important to you. Bill Hybels refers to this as holy discontent, a sort of God-given righteous indignation that can be great fuel for changing the world.[9]

Answer some of the following questions to better understand the causes closest to your heart:

Causes Assessment

What makes you angry about the state of the world? (Go back and look at chapter 1. Which reality is most troubling to you?)

What are you most afraid of for the next generation, whether you have children or not?

What news stories tick you off the most?

What do you want to change in the world for the better?

Each part of this personal inventory is an attempt to help you see your role in God's world. I love to look across my own church and see the vastly different causes, concerns, and passions reflected in our congregation. And remember not to be a cause snob. Others will feel as passionately about other causes as you do about yours. Cheer them on!

4. Possibilities versus Limits

Finally, we need to identify our limits in order to acknowledge our realistic constraints while also dreaming beyond them. Limitations and circumstances don't have to be negative vision-busters. They can offer us direction about where to begin responding to the vast needs of the world. But I prefer to start with the blue-sky approach by dreaming wildly about the possibilities, and then to scale the dream back as needed. Forget your limits for a minute!

Dreaming without Limits

What would you love to do or accomplish before you die? Try to make the list as big as you can.

What would you do if you couldn't fail? If there were no fear of failure, what would you do?

What would you do if you weren't limited by money, education, age, and so on?

These kinds of questions help us dream without immediately assuming limitations. There's a strong possibility that the kinds of things you wrote above are things you really want to do. Now come back the other way and consider realistic limitations:

• • • • • • Dreaming within Limits • • • • • •

What specific objections or barriers do you anticipate from moving toward some of the things you're discovering?

What are some of your life circumstances (for example, family, health, finances, and so on) that significantly shape how you live out your calling?

Understanding your boundaries might be the very tool you need to best live out your calling. Think about the long-term impact of the apostle Paul's calling because of his frequent imprisonments. It's unlikely we would have many of his writings apart from his time spent behind bars. I'm not trivializing this hardship in his life. But we're wise to pay careful attention to how the challenges in our own lives are often connected to living out our calling.

It isn't necessary to answer every question in this inventory. But these four categories—personality, skills/expertise, causes, and possibilities versus limits—are the most important themes for you to consider as you discern how to join God's redemptive work globally. Now as you go back and see what you've written, think about these questions: What themes emerge? Where do you feel confused? What do you need to explore further? Take your time, pray, reflect, observe, and then be sure to involve the people closest to you as an essential part of this journey.

COMMUNAL AUTHORITY

Left to ourselves, we can come up with some pretty skewed perceptions of how we're supposed to partner with God in the world. As we go through this discernment process, it's essential to involve the people who know us best. And we're not simply asking for their input so we can pick and choose from their advice as we please. What does it look like to surrender our decisions to a community that exercises some authority over us?

Linda and I are committed to living in community with a few other individuals and couples. We make decisions together about our finances, where to live, our parenting, our jobs, and how to get involved in various causes. We aren't living out of a common purse or under the same roof, but this is more than just going to one another for advice. It's about trusting our community with the decisions facing us.

There are times when I question whether our community is making the right choice about something that affects me very personally. In one case, it was as simple as submitting to the community's decision for me to decline a speaking invitation. Another time, it was as major as turning down a job offer that seemed ideal. But even in those times when I don't agree with the community's decision, I find great protection and discipline in surrendering my choices to the godly community of which I'm part. They love me for who I am and often help me see things I miss. And I must say, in retrospect, I'm really glad I didn't end up in what I thought was my dream job.[10]

Identify the significant relationships in your life. Talk through your personal inventory with these people and listen carefully for how they affirm or disaffirm what you've discovered. Schedule time with friends, family members, and colleagues to discuss you, and just you. Ask them to name your strengths and weaknesses, or your talents and abilities, as they see them.

The Quaker community has a custom called a "clearness committee" which weds personal discovery with community. The clearness committee is a process whereby a group refrains from giving you advice but spends three hours asking honest, open-ended questions to help you discover who you are and what you should do. We shouldn't cloister ourselves to discern calling, nor can we delegate the work to someone else. Instead, together with our community, we need to seek how to engage in what God has uniquely created us to do.[11]

EXPERIMENT

It's time to try a taste test. Go on a short-term missions trip that's connected to some of your interests and skills. Be ready to serve wherever you go, but make the emphasis of your trip *learning*. Every community has needs you can probably help meet. And every community has resources that may surprisingly meet needs in *your* life. Try to make this type of reciprocal giving and receiving a part of how you engage in serving others.

Consider other ways to tap into some of your skills, interests, and dreams. Take a class, apply for a part-time job, volunteer, help a friend at a job that interests you, or attend lectures or forums that address some of your global concerns. Talk with other people who are engaging in a cause, and see how their experience resonates with what you observed through your personal inventory.

Consider whether a bolder move such as quitting your job and going overseas for a year might be a viable option for you. Into what existing commitments should you lean more fully, and from which ones should you pull away? Again, don't make these decisions alone.

You don't have to be certain about whether this is *the* cause or issue before giving it a try. As you get involved in it, either you'll want to stay with it and grow your knowledge and experience or you'll quickly lose interest and move on to something else. And remember: you aren't deciding this for life. Our passions and interests evolve and change, because we're constantly changing and growing. Think, pray, and try something!

THE NEXT RIGHT STEP

Most of us won't figure out all at once exactly how we should engage globally. Start small, but don't just sit around waiting for it all to come together. One of my friends consistently asks me, "What's the *next* right thing?" I'm a futurist, so I don't really like her question. I want to know where I'm heading over the next ten years, and because of this tendency, I often miss ways I can make a difference *now*. Love the one in front of you. You aren't going to wipe out AIDS in one day. Look for the people and circumstances right under your nose. What's the next right step?

That's not a rhetorical question. Stop and answer it right now!

What Now?

What's the next right step?

When will I do this?

Take responsibility for how you're going to get involved, but hold your ideas and plans loosely. Only God sees the big picture, but we've been given the opportunity to responsibly and diligently join God in making the world a better place today. Consider joining millions of Christians in making the Shakertown Pledge. This was written in 1973 by a group of Christians near Lexington, Kentucky, as a commitment to respond to the inequitable distribution of resources around the world. Since then, millions of Christians around the world have vowed:

1. I declare myself to be a world citizen.
2. I commit myself to lead an ecologically sound life.
3. I commit myself to lead a life of creative simplicity and to share my personal wealth with the world's poor.
4. I commit myself to join with others in reshaping institutions in order to bring about a more just global society in which each person has full access to the needed resources for their physical, emotional, intellectual, and spiritual growth.
5. I commit myself to occupational accountability, and in so doing I will seek to avoid the creation of products which cause harm to others.
6. I affirm the gift of my body, and commit myself to its proper nourishment and physical well-being.
7. I commit myself to examine continually my relations with

others, and to attempt to relate honestly, morally, and lovingly to those around me.

8. I commit myself to personal renewal through prayer, meditation, and study.
9. I commit myself to responsible participation in a community of faith.[12]

This is how we were created to live. Grace and peace to you as you seek to discover where your life intersects with what God is doing all over the world. Yes, you.

CHAPTER 11

OUR JOURNEY

DISCERNING OUR CONTRIBUTION TOGETHER

When I say the word *missionary*, who do you picture? That simple word conjures up all kinds of images for me. For many years, *missionary* usually meant a lone couple or individual who spent a lot of years going to Bible college, raising support, and learning a foreign language. They packed all their belongings into a container, and off they'd go for the rest of their lives to serve God in some exotic, scary place. We heard from them at conferences, like the one where I decided to be a missionary. They shared cool stories about life in the jungle and autographed our Bibles (what was up with that?!). In my mind, these people were on the top rung of the spiritual ladder. You couldn't be more godly or spiritual than a missionary. And quite honestly, some of them seemed a little weird. Their sense of humor and fashion seemed a bit quirky and unique.

I'm often struck by the thought of how differently my girls understand *mission* and *missionary* compared with my understanding at their age. Like them, I grew up in a Christian home and went to church within days of leaving my mother's womb. But nowadays *missionary* might just as well refer to someone working with Arabic-speaking people outside Detroit as to someone moving to the Middle East. Missionaries aren't just planting churches in Mexico and Eastern Europe; they're reaching out to international students at nearby universities and befriending seasonal farmworkers in rural Midwest communities. Missions has become the work of everyday Christians and churches. And on the whole, I think this changed understanding and increased accessibility of missions is a really good thing.

My aim in this book has been to expand your view of global mission to make it even broader. Mission includes Christian businesspeople working nine-to-five jobs, Christian teachers in inner-city and suburban schools, and Christian baristas at local coffee shops engaging in global mission right where they are. Some missions experts will argue that we should reserve the term *missionary* for those who move cross-culturally to fill a more traditional role of vocational ministry. I'll leave that debate for others. As we've seen, we're all called to be priests, invited to *partner with God to work in the world.* This is what we were created to do, and it's something that's best done together with others in the body of Christ. So how does a church or any group of believers discern how to work in concert with one another to make a difference in the world? The questions we examined in the last chapter apply equally well here. Let's begin by learning how to respond to God's invitation *together*, and then we'll review a discernment process for groups.

THE CHURCH AS MISSIONARY

Bob Roberts, pastor of Northwood Church in Dallas, says a missionary is not an individual; it's a *church*. He believes that local churches are called together to reach certain people and places and address specific issues in the world. And in the same spirit that this book has been written in, he asks the question, What better way to engage in global mission than through the jobs people hold? He understands his role to be more than getting people in the pews to engage in "pay and pray missions." Instead his gauge as a pastor is, How many laypeople am I mobilizing? The best missional strategy for a church sits in the pew. The number and diversity of vocations, passions, skills, and interests of the people in a church determine the strategy's scope.[1]

Growing in faith and responding to the needs of the world are intended to happen together with others, not individually. The majority of the time, when the word *you* appears in the New Testament, it refers to a *plural* audience, not to an individual person. Ultimately, the real meaning of our lives isn't found in our personal pursuit of following Jesus and individually changing the world. Instead it's realized as all of us, God's people worldwide, live intentionally as God's partners. There are both personal and communal implications to all of this. When I fail to live as God intended for me to live, I hold others back. And when others in the body of Christ make good, healthy choices, they help me along in my journey. This communal emphasis is counterintuitive to the individualistic obsession of our Western culture. But as we live out our calling together, both in local communities of faith and spiritually with Christians everywhere, we will begin to experience authentic and sustainable transformation.

Churches that take on the role of missionary will encounter some challenges. To a large degree, the church has lost its moral authority in many places around the world. Certainly, that's true among the dominant culture in North America. The countless scandals and hypocrisy among Christian leaders have made many North Americans skeptical toward organized Christianity and religion in general. Society used to look to the church for cues on how to respond to a crisis. In the midst of economic recession, people looked to the church for help and guidance. If kids were killing themselves, the church was there to help. During times of war, the church was viewed as a place to get an informed response. Now if an idea comes from the church, it seems to undermine the cause at hand, or at the very least the church's view seems irrelevant. And I'm not sure we even believe in our own authority anymore. We're happy to let governmental agencies and other groups care for the issues of the world.

Once, when my church was laying out our vision for responding to the cries of our world, a church member asked, "But isn't this the U.N.'s job?!"

Although we've had our share of failures and mistakes as the church of Jesus, it's still an amazing fact that the church has carried the gospel across two millennia and thousands of cultures and civilizations—all the way to you and me! The church is the ideal agent for changing the world. Many of our local churches simply need some realignment to maximize their potential.

William Schweiker from the University of Chicago Divinity School suggests that the main task of churches is to witness to God's reign by teaching, learning, and living justice. According to Schweiker, whenever we find Eden-like goodness in the world, we ought to embrace it and find ways to join what's there. Movements like the One campaign, corporate social responsibility, and environmental stewardship are redemptive causes we should support and join. And when we encounter evil in our world and experience firsthand the fallen nature of our society, we must work in partnership with others to bring transformation and hope. Adopting unwanted babies, mentoring fatherless high school students, and fighting racism are just a few ways we can demonstrate God's reign and transforming power in the world. As we *become* living pictures of justice in the world, we might also find ourselves regaining moral credibility.[2]

COMMUNITY INVENTORY

Again, however, the question comes up: where should we get involved, with whom, and in what ways? How do we choose? How should we organize ourselves to do what God is revealing to us? The remainder of this chapter provides some initial questions and exercises for discerning how to get engaged globally as a local congregation or even as a group of friends or a family. I've written the process for use in a church setting, with a mission team, or with a small group, but it can easily be used by other types of groups as well. Most of the questions will apply to any group context. A youth leader can substitute the phrase "youth ministry" for "church," and a small group can do the same.

Begin with prayer. Pray together often. Go slow. Spend extended time over some great food, conversation, laughter, and prayer, exploring how to get involved as a community. Don't let the leader hole up in a room and figure this out for the rest of the group. Share the discovery process. You can use this process to discern your shared calling as a family, small group, youth ministry, local church, or any kind of group.

Ruth Haley-Barton, a noted author on spiritual direction, has done a great deal to help congregations discern what God is doing and how to be part of it. Her book *Sacred Rhythms* is a great resource, with a number of practical exercises and guidelines you can use. I've adapted a few of her ideas for the following exercise in communal discernment. Spending time together in prayer and discernment is a great way for your group to prepare for a wider inventory of how to get engaged globally together.

Discerning Together

Introduction

Read aloud together Acts 17:27–28: "[God] is not far from any one of us. 'For in him we live and move and have our being.'"

Spend two to three minutes silently reflecting on these words of Paul.

End the silence by reading this passage again: "[God] is not far from any one of us. 'For in him we live and move and have our being.'"

Ask

Ask the Spirit to prepare you as a group for this time of conversation with Jesus. God's presence is here with us.

Give everyone time to ask the Spirit to prepare their hearts.

Examine Yourselves

Read 2 Corinthians 13:5: "Examine yourselves to see whether you are living in the faith; test yourselves.... Christ Jesus is in you."

Think through the last twenty-four hours:

- Where did you fail?

- When did you love?

- What patterns (good or bad) do you see in your life?

- Where did you observe evil (near or far)?

Find God in All Things

Read Deuteronomy 30:14–15, 19: "The Word [of God] is very near to you, it is in your mouth and in your heart so you may obey it. See, I set before you today life and prosperity, death and destruction. . . . Choose life."

- Where did you see God today?

- To what does your mind keep wandering while you sit here in silence?

Reflect

- Individual: What struck you or demanded your attention?

- Small Group: Share with a few others how you feel about this discernment process we've just begun.

- Large Group: What did we experience here today? What was discerned through this time together?

"Discernment is the capacity to sense what God is doing and the decision to join in it."[3]

After Jacob's dream at Bethel, the next morning he says, "Surely the Lord is in this place, and I was not aware of it" (Gen. 28:16).

God is here among us. We want to heighten our awareness of what he's doing and how we can join him.

- What does this mean for us? What is God calling us to do?

- Who is God calling us to be?

1. Roots

The journey toward communal discernment begins by studying our roots. We stand on the shoulders of faithful Christians who have gone before us—both in our local churches and in the worldwide Christian church. Consider the long line of generations that have struggled to follow Jesus before us in places throughout the world.

The Scriptures are the best place to begin exploring our roots. The Bible is a cacophony of voices, inspired by God, with poems, stories, letters, and accounts of people responding to God's gracious invitation to partner with him in saving the world. As we say at my church, "To know where we're going, we have to know where we've been."[4]

Next we need to spend time reflecting on the roots of our own Christian community. Whether our church has been around for six months or 160 years, we need to return to the roots of our local body as part of discovering our role in the world.

If you don't know these details, ask around. This is a great excuse to include some of the long-term members in the discernment process. People like me find this to be really hard work, because I'm far more interested in looking forward than in looking backward. But others are better wired for looking back and remembering the past. Reflect on your past together through the following exercise and questions:

• • • • • Beginning to Present Timeline • • • • •

Complete a timeline for the church, starting from the very beginning:

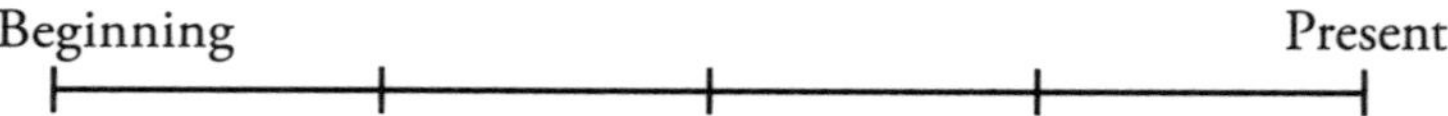

What's the story behind how our church began?

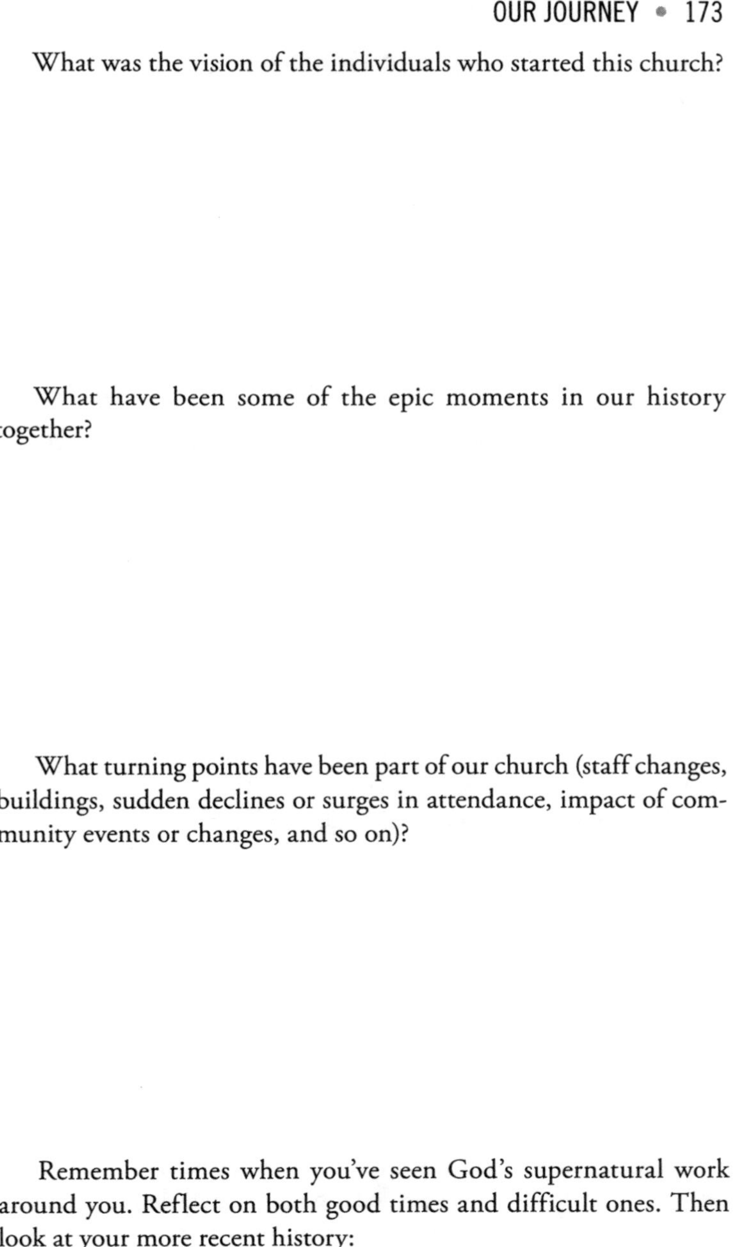

What was the vision of the individuals who started this church?

What have been some of the epic moments in our history together?

What turning points have been part of our church (staff changes, buildings, sudden declines or surges in attendance, impact of community events or changes, and so on)?

Remember times when you've seen God's supernatural work around you. Reflect on both good times and difficult ones. Then look at your more recent history:

Last Eighteen Months Timeline

Complete a timeline for the last eighteen months of life together.

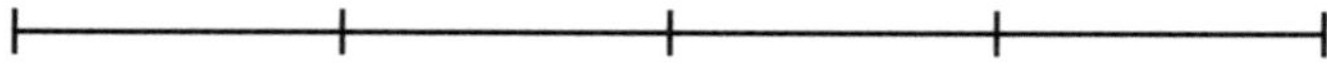

What's been happening over the last year that merits our attention?

What do we anticipate in the near future?

As you look at both timelines, consider: What are some of the unique characteristics of your local body? What's been consistent throughout your history? What's been inconsistent?

Then spend some time exploring the roots of your missional involvement. What's been the primary nature of how you've served locally and globally? Some things you might consider are the degree to which your missional involvement, if any, has included the following (check all that apply):

Missional Roots

- ☐ Local more than international
- ☐ International more than local
- ☐ Denominationally determined
- ☐ Crisis driven (for example, responding to a tsunami or earthquake)
- ☐ Shaped by a pastor or key leader
- ☐ Responsive to requests
- ☐ Primarily financially driven
- ☐ Heavy emphasis on short-term missions trips
- ☐ Missionary dependent
- ☐ Other: ______________________________

Don't rush through this process. A thoughtful reminiscing about your roots can play a revealing role in helping you discern how to collectively engage in mission.

2. Current Reality

Looking at your present reality is just as important as looking at your roots. What's going on currently that needs attention? What realities—good, bad, or neutral—are facing us right now? What passions are shared among our community? What relationships have come together that are worthy of our consideration?

One of the most effective ways of assessing reality and anticipating the future is to use the familiar Strengths, Weaknesses, Opportunities, and Threats (SWOT) assessment. Do at least two SWOT analyses—one for your church as a whole and one that specifically assesses your missional involvement (locally and/or globally). These assessments are best completed together as a group. Brainstorm as many responses as possible for each of the four areas (sidebar, p. 176).

Assessing Our Reality

Strengths	Weaknesses
What are the positive characteristics of our current situation? What assets do we have—both hard, tangible assets like finances, buildings, or numbers of people and soft assets like high morale or certain skill sets?	What are the most challenging situations and dynamics currently facing us? What liabilities do we have—again, both hard liabilities (e.g., debt and decline in attendance) and soft ones (e.g., a vacuum of leadership or a growing spirit of disunity)?
Opportunities	**Threats**
Where are we seeing potential for growth and progress? What benefits might occur as we more fully define our group's role in global mission?	What future challenges might likely come our way? What circumstances might cause us to struggle to pursue global mission?

3. People

Calling should emerge from the people and relationships that are part of your church. It's tempting to start with what's most important to the senior leader or with a trendy issue getting a lot of press, but start the discernment process with people. Who's part of your church? What's important to them? To whom and what are you naturally connected through your people? Here are two ways to think through the people-related issues: (1) connections and relationships and (2) vocations and skills.

Connections and Relationships

Pay attention to the connections and relationships that exist within your church, the community where you live, and the networks to which you're connected. Answer the following:

• • • • Our Connections and Relationships • • • •

What large populations of people from other parts of the world live nearby?

What refugee communities have settled here?

What ethnic groups are represented in our church?

Through our networks, what natural connections do we have with particular peoples, places, languages, and issues near and far?

With whom are we partnered organizationally? With what missionaries and indigenous pastors are we connected? Which of these seem to have the most promise?

We tend to become like the people with whom we share a cup of coffee. Typically, the issues that matter to our friends become the issues that matter to us, and vice versa. Pay attention to the shared concerns, connections, and relationships that exist among you. Sometimes connections surface as you simply become more aware of the people and relationships around you. Noah Filipiak, a pastor in Lansing, Michigan, had been challenging his church to join him in praying about adopting a local refugee family. Noah expected to do this by partnering with another organization, but one of his church members got ahead of him by merely striking up a conversation with two Nepali women on the city bus who had recently moved to their community. Suddenly a group of people in Lansing were learning how to play cricket, eating curried lentils together, and talking about Christianity and Hinduism. Don't miss the grassroots connections that emerge.

Social networking sites have awakened us to the wide reach that exists even among a small group of people. Pay attention to your collective networks, relationships, and shared concerns.

Vocations and Skills

In the same way we inventoried our personal skills and interests, we need to look at the collective skills, experiences, and interests throughout our community.

Our Vocations and Skills

What types of vocations and careers are represented in our congregation? Do we have an unusual predominance of some careers?

What specialized skills are featured in our body?

Do we have proximity with a particular industry, in a way that might shape how we should engage locally and globally?

When I was a mission pastor, our church had an unusually high percentage of physicians, dentists, and nurses. And we had some natural connections to Thailand through some church members from there. This led to a partnership that included medical care for the Akha and Lahu tribes in Northern Thailand. The existing relationships, skills, and specializations reflected in your church body can be a cue toward how best to engage globally as a community.

4. Causes and Issues

Usually, certain causes, issues, and people groups surface when you are looking carefully at who is part of your church. If not, some will emerge as you walk through the questions and exercises in this chapter. Spend time studying different parts of the world. What are the various issues and needs there? Which have the best fit with your church?

A variety of groups and agencies exist to provide information and connections globally. Be sure they know you aren't just interested in finding somewhere to channel money or a place to take a missions trip. You're in the driver's seat of discerning how your church engages locally and globally. So use missions organizations to help *your church* fulfill your missional calling, not vice versa.

God is at work everywhere. Pay attention and discern how to be part of it. Have your group assess the priority you want to place on the following:

Prioritizing Issues and Causes

One way to use a list like this is to gather your core group and give everyone fifteen votes they can use however they wish (for example, they can give five votes to one issue and spread the other ten among four to five other issues). Vote accordingly:

- ☐ Hands-on involvement from the congregation
- ☐ Working with a particular agency with whom you have history and/or relationship
- ☐ Children
- ☐ Church planting
- ☐ Community development
- ☐ Evangelism
- ☐ A specific region or location
- ☐ People-group focused
- ☐ Leadership development
- ☐ Short-term missions trips
- ☐ More support for fewer missionaries
- ☐ Support of local, indigenous pastors and leaders
- ☐ Raising up missionaries in our midst
- ☐ Developing sister-church relationships
- ☐ Poor and oppressed
- ☐ Social justice
- ☐ Specific issues (for example, water, HIV/AIDS, microfinance, and those listed in chapter 1): ________________________
- ☐ Other: ____________________________________

How do we even begin to make decisions about which issues and causes we should support together? Economist Bjorn Lomborg has devoted his work to helping people prioritize the global issues that are of paramount importance to us and future generations. His provocative TED Talk on the best way to spend fifty billion dollars in the world is well worth watching.[5] Learn from experts like Lomborg and others to aid in the prioritization of issues and causes you should join.

And pay attention to the people, places, and issues with which your group feels the most chemistry. Don't underestimate the importance of this. Spend a great deal of time talking about it together and praying. Is your interest sustained and growing? You don't want to get everyone motivated and then find yourselves bored with what you've chosen. I can't emphasize this enough. Pay attention to the affinity your group has with various options. Although this shouldn't be the only way you decide where and with whom to be involved, it should be a significant part of your decision.

CHOOSE

Having inventoried your roots, current reality, people, and potential causes, narrow down the options. On the one hand, there's no need to rush this. Take your time. But sometimes we wait too long or we overspiritualize the process. The tendency one way or the other may largely depend on the personality and culture of the group. At some point, you need to pick something and go for it!

In light of what we discover in this clarifying process, we need to go through a refinement of our church programming. If your church is already engaged in several ways missionally, it's important for you to bring focus to what you're doing. If you aren't doing anything globally, pick somewhere to start. What picture emerges as you consider the various areas we've explored in this chapter? Bathe this in prayer, learning, and conversation and begin to serve!

The exercises in this chapter are just the initial steps toward discerning how to get involved together. Other books describe a more robust process for churches to discern and implement a plan for their local and global involvement (for example, see Catalyst's manual *Your FOCUS on the World*). But the questions and exercises we've covered are a good starting point for discovering where and how we can join together to make a difference in the world.

WAKE UP!

The church is Christ's presence in the world today. Some have even suggested that the trendy term *missional church* is redundant. If a church isn't missional, it isn't really a church. I welcome the renewed emphasis on mission that has come out of the missional church movement, and I think we're wise to remember that without engagement in mission, serious questions should be raised as to whether a so-called church is really a church at all. Mission is something we're all invited into together. It's central to our calling as the people of God.

There's little hope of making a real difference in the world as a solo agent of God. The only way to live this out is with the other people God has put into our lives. None of us can pull this off alone, but in community we can join God's redemptive cause!

So who is God calling us to be? What is God calling us to do together? Look at the people God has put around you and together with them discover how to serve the causes big and small, near and far, deep and wide! And watch how God continues to be made flesh through Christians all over the world.

The church is a sleeping giant, possessing the resurrected power of Jesus — a power that can meet the deepest, darkest aches and groans of our global village. In calling the Ephesian believers to see the opportunities right in front of them, Paul quotes what is widely believed to be a first-century poem or hymn: " 'Wake up, sleeper, rise from the dead, and Christ will shine on you' " (Eph. 5:14). He goes on to say, "Be very careful, then, how you live — not as unwise but as wise, making the most of every opportunity, because the days are evil" (vv. 15 – 16).

It's time for the church to wake up and embrace our calling as priests and to partner with God to redeem our world through the life-giving love of Jesus.

CONCLUSION

Several years have passed since Linda and I sat shell-shocked in our living room after watching *Hotel Rwanda*. We often have days and even weeks when we become so consumed with the demands of our own lives that we give little thought to how we can help our global neighbors. But it's never long before we're reminded about the things going on in our global village, and then we stop to talk about how we're doing from our little corner of the world.

We're not trying to save the world all by ourselves. But neither can we turn a blind eye to the needs we've seen up close. We're just trying to do our part. God invites each of us to do our part in making the world a better place.

Don't underestimate what God *is* doing and can continue to do through your life. Yes, you! You might be surprised which kids from the Little League team you coach end up pursuing something globally significant. Don't discount the difference you can make holding a Romanian orphan in your arms, or washing the stumps of people affected by leprosy, or faithfully sharing Christ with an antagonistic neighbor. When we align our lives with redemptive causes, God promises to do far more than we could begin to ask or imagine! (See Eph. 3:20–21.) Slowly but surely, God is ushering in a whole new world.

One time I was in Kenya with a group of East African pastors, and we were trying to imagine the conversations we'd have in the new heaven and the new earth. Several described their desire to talk with Old Testament heroes like Abraham, Daniel, and Deborah and ask, "What was it like to be part of God's people back then?" Another leader said she couldn't wait to sit down with Mary and ask her, "What was it like to hold Jesus and then follow him all the way to the cross?" Still others wanted to hear firsthand about Pentecost and life in the first-century church. "What was it like to be where it all started?" That was the recurring question. After several minutes of this, the elder statesman of the group, Bishop James from Uganda, stood up. He said nothing for several seconds, and then with his eyes closed he said, "Ah, my dear brothers and sisters. I don't see it like this at all. You see, when I imagine walking through the pearly gates, I envision all these Bible heroes running up to me and asking, 'James. What was it like? What was it like to be living in the twenty-first-century world, when there were followers of Jesus in every nation? What was it like to be part of a worldwide movement of God's people working together to reverse the curse of evil? What was it like to experience on such a grand scale what we knew only in seed form?'"

James's comments got me thinking about the unprecedented time period in which we're living. Never before has the revolutionary work of God in and through the church been so immediately evident. When you're part of the church of Jesus Christ, you're part of a worldwide movement that can never be stopped. We're on our way to a new heaven and a new earth, where we will once again live entirely as we were intended to live. It's mind-boggling to think about what life on the new earth will look like. Will there be a better Beethoven? Will we see better Rembrandts, read better poetry, and discover new technological advances? Will geologists continue to explore the treasures of the earth, and will architects continue to build imposing and attractive structures? We don't know.[1] But what we do know is that we will once again perfectly image God and live in a world completely filled with peace, harmony, and wholeness. God will be magnified by our work in ways that will surpass our wildest dreams. But we don't have to wait for eternity to get started on this. Let's get at it now—living as we were created to live, bringing heaven's presence to earth, and responding to the groans for redemption all across the globe.

With the church mothers, we pray, "O Spirit of the LORD, rest on us this day, as we ponder the mystery of the vision you hold out to us. It seems impossible that a wolf and a lamb, a leopard and a kid, a calf and a young lion, could be playmates, let alone a child place its hand in an adder's lair and not be harmed. And yet you call each of us to reconcile whatever lamb and wolf, kid and leopard, lion and calf are represented by aspects of our own personalities, so that we in turn can believe it possible for humans to live in peace with each other in our world. Show us the way of this just rule of your reign in our hearts, that we may be instruments of that reign wherever you send us. We ask this in your name Immanuel, God-with-us. Amen."[2]

God is inviting you to make the world a better place. Go do it.

Yes, you.

APPENDIX

FAQs

I've had the privilege of interacting with many different people about the issues in this book. Part of my own calling is to come alongside leaders and help them see what's going on in the world and suggest ways to effectively respond. As I've done so, I continually encounter some of the same questions, a few of which I've included here.

Q: A lot of these examples don't really seem like "missions." Aren't these people just doing their jobs well and living their lives?

A: Exactly! That's the whole point. Mission work has too often been segmented as this separate task that gets done by special people or only during short-term missions trips. But with some intentionality, most of the things we do in life can be oriented toward meeting the needs of the world. Our work, relationships, studies, buying habits, voting, and much more are all related to living as God's partners in the world.

Q: What about full-time ministry? Isn't there a place for some who devote their vocational and career interests to full-time service as pastors, missionaries, or other kinds of ministry leaders?

A: Absolutely! We've all been called to engage in mission as what we were created to do. But some of us are sent by our communities into what are typically called "full-time ministry roles." The primary orientation of those serving in these roles should be equipping other Christians to live out mission in their contexts.

The danger is in thinking that those working for churches or Christian organizations are the only ones doing true full-time service. John Stott, one of the foremost leaders in the modern evangelical movement, writes, "We often give the impression that if a young Christian man is really keen for Christ, he will undoubtedly become a foreign missionary, that if he is not quite keen as that, he will stay home and become a pastor, that if he lacks the dedication to be a pastor, he will no doubt serve as a doctor or teacher, while those who end up in social work or the media or (worst of all) in politics are not far removed from serious backsliding."[1]

There should be no upper and lower class of Christian ministry. Every Christian has a high calling. The business leader, the lawyer, the student, and the factory worker can all do God's work (or fail to do it) just as much as the minister and the missionary.[2]

Q: Why did you include in the book examples from people and organizations that don't identify themselves as Christians?

A: Christians should be among the greatest advocates for peace and goodness in the world. But all kinds of people and groups long for shalom, justice, truth, beauty, and delight. A person doesn't have to believe in Christ to unconsciously do a part of Christ's work in the world. Neil Plantinga of Calvin Theological Seminary writes, "God needn't employ only Christian organizations to push forward the cause of the kingdom. God can use all kinds of groups and persons to further his purposes, including groups and persons that are uninterested in God or even opposed to God."[3] Some of these individuals offer great examples of what it means to serve the world's deepest needs through their work. What I'm calling for is the *conscious*, intentional use of our work, relationships, and everything we do as Christians to be part of God's redemptive work in the world to restore complete shalom.

Q: How do you decide whether to focus on local needs or global needs?

A: The distinctions between local and global are getting more difficult to make all the time. Everywhere is a part of everywhere.

The term *glocal* has been a helpful way of demonstrating that the things we do locally have a global impact and the things going on in another part of the world affect us locally.

Most anything you get engaged in has a local and global dimension to it. That's been evident throughout the book. We're more aware of human trafficking in places like Southeast Asia, but trafficking goes on in most North American cities and towns too. There are people with HIV and AIDS at home and in places around the world. People all over the globe are in need of redemption and love — poor and rich, young and old, famous and infamous.

There's an important ethical principle called moral proximity, the idea that we care most about the joys and sorrows of those close to us. There's something wrong with the dad who pours himself into mentoring young men on skid row while ignoring his own children. There's a reason why local newscasts always report on the people from our community affected by a tragedy far away. Our priestly service must begin with those living near, a proximity which can include familiarity, kinship, and closeness in terms of time and space. On the other hand, the interdependence created by our technology-fueled, globalized world heightens our responsibility for our fellow image bearers far away — those living on the other side of the world and the generations who will follow us. As you discern the people, places, and issues to which you've been called, look for how to engage both near and far.

Q: *All this concern about the poor and oppressed is great, but what about the gospel and evangelism? Don't we run the risk of doing all kinds of good in the world without ever telling people about Jesus?*

A: The North American church has spent too much energy debating the proclamation of the gospel versus the so-called social gospel. Many in the Christian church in other parts of the world laugh at the thought that the gospel could be one without the other. In fairness, the concerns are that on the one hand, if we merely preach the gospel, people may hear a theoretical description of who Jesus is without experiencing any of the realities of who Jesus is. On the other hand, are compassion and service enough?

The gospel must be both proclaimed in *word* and lived in *deed*. When John's disciples came to Jesus asking, "Are you the one?" Jesus replied, "Tell John what you have seen and heard." Jesus proclaimed *words* that were authenticated by his *deeds*—through the blind seeing, cripples walking, lepers being cleansed, deaf hearing, and the dead being raised.

We must faithfully call people to follow Jesus as the best possible way to live. We cannot neglect our responsibility to faithfully announce, *"Repent! The kingdom is at hand."* But the words of the gospel must also be expressed in ways that demonstrate the good news of Jesus. Our words work in tandem with our deeds. Any gospel message that doesn't exemplify the reign of God over poverty, disease, racism, war, divorce, and financial strain isn't good news!

Q: Aren't most efforts to combat global poverty pointless because of all the corrupt governments?

A: People sometimes shrug off the value of getting involved in changing the quality of life for people in various parts of the world because of the corrupt governments that preside. The sense is, What's the point of sending aid to developing countries when corrupt governments will just use it for evil purposes?

You hear this sentiment from people like Bill O'Reilly of Fox News, who declared, "Africa is a corrupt continent; it's a continent in chaos."[4] O'Reilly is convinced that any aid given to Africa is just going right down the drain. He says, "Africa is corrupt and riddled with authoritarianism. It lacks modern values and the institutions of the free market economy needed to achieve success. In fact, Africa's morals are so broken down that it's no surprise AIDS has run out of control."[5]

The opposing view is more utopian in nature and says, "These governments aren't so bad. Each nation should be free to determine their own development strategies, so don't attach strings to the ways you get involved." As usual, there's truth in both extremes of this argument. There are many corrupt, dysfunctional governments that exist across much of the developing world. Granted, my own government is far from an exemplary model when you consider recent cases of violating the human rights of prisoners, and the out-of-control financing of political campaigns by special interest groups. The truth is, there's both good and bad governing going on in the United States—and the same is true around the world. There are capable, honest, and well-meaning leaders in almost every government, and incompetent, corrupt ones. Economist William Easterly writes, "Over a couple decades of working on developing countries, I have met outstanding government officials from every continent, whom I admire greatly. These officials complain more knowledgeably about bad politics and corruption in their own countries than outsiders can.... But we must face reality—decades of research by social scientists, not to mention everyday observation, show just how dysfunctional government can get in many countries.... We don't do the poor any favors by tenderly respecting the sensitivities of bad rulers who oppress their own people."[6]

It's unhelpful to go to either extreme—overlooking bad governments in places throughout the world or embracing a stereotype of all governments in developing countries as always bad or ineffective. The same is true of the age-old concern about giving money to a homeless person. I was taught for years that I shouldn't give money to someone who might take it just to go and buy their next fix. But I don't see that kind of cautious giving in Jesus. Jesus didn't stop healing blind people for fear their restored sight might cause them to lust. He doesn't stop giving me good opportunities for fear I'll become arrogant.

I mentioned earlier that wise assessment and measurement of outcomes is important. It's appropriate to wrestle with these questions. There are no simple answers.

• • •

These are five-cent answers to million-dollar questions. I don't intend to reduce the complexity of these issues too much. But hopefully, my responses will stir you to ask more questions and continue to explore how to best serve from your own backyard. I'd love to interact with you about these issues and others at my blog (*www.davidlivermore.com/blog*).

NOTES

Chapter 1

1. Donella Meadows, "Who Lives in the Global Village?" Technical Report (Hartland, Vt.: Sustainability Institute, 2005).
2. United Nations Programme on HIV/AIDS (UNAIDS) and World Health Organization (WHO), *AIDS Epidemic Update 2007*, Switzerland, 2007.
3. Centers for Disease Control and Prevention, "Tuberculosis," *www.cdc.gov/tb/* (June 3, 2009).
4. U.S. Department of State Office to Monitor and Combat Trafficking in Persons, "U.S. Department of State: Trafficking in Persons Report," U.S. Department of State, *www.state.gov/g/tip/rls/tiprpt/2008/105376.htm* (accessed June 15, 2009).
5. Stop the Traffik, "The Chocolate Campaign," *www.stopthetraffik.org/getInvolved/act/chocolate/chocolate.aspx* (accessed May 10, 2009).
6. Thomas Friedman, *The World Is Flat: A Brief History of the Twenty-First Century* (New York: Farrar, Straus & Giroux, 2005), 3.
7. Fareed Zakaria, *The Post-American World* (New York: Norton, 2008), 91.
8. Ibid., 135–36.
9. David Barrett and Todd Johnson, eds., *World Christian Trends: AD 30–AD 2200* (Pasadena, Calif.: William Carey Library, 2001), 17.
10. Ibid.
11. L. A. Braskamp, D. C. Braskamp, and K. C. Merrill, "Global Perspective Inventory (GPI): Its Purpose, Construction, Potential Uses, and Psychometric Characteristics," 2008, Global Perspective Institute, *http://gpi.central.edu/* (accessed July 2, 2009).

Chapter 2

1. Rob Bell, "The Importance of Beginning in the Beginning" (sermon delivered at Mars Hill Bible Church, Grandville, Mich., August 16, 2009).
2. Anthony Hoekema, *Created in God's Image* (Grand Rapids, Mich.: Eerdmans, 1986), 67.
3. James Grier, "Image of God" (lecture delivered to a Christian ethics class, Grand Rapids Theological Seminary, Grand Rapids, Mich., May 15, 1991).
4. N. T. Wright, *Following Jesus: Biblical Reflections on Discipleship* (Grand Rapids, Mich.: Eerdmans, 1994), 10.

5. R. Paul Stevens, *Seven Days of Faith: Every Day Alive with God* (Colorado Springs: NavPress, 2001), 21.
6. Hoekema, *Created in God's Image*, 73–74.
7. Michael VanHorn, "Christian Worldview: Humans and Creation in the Plan of God" (unpublished paper, June 1992).
8. N. T. Wright, *The Resurrection of the Son of God* (Minneapolis: Fortress Press, 2003), 290.
9. Hoekema, *Created in God's Image*, 81.
10. Richard Mouw, *When the Kings Come Marching In* (Grand Rapids, Mich.: Eerdmans, 1983), 47.
11. Brian J. Walsh and J. Richard Middleton, *The Transforming Vision: Shaping a Christian World View* (Downers Grove, Ill.: InterVarsity Press, 1984), 97.
12. N. T. Wright, *Surprised by Hope: Rethinking Heaven, the Resurrection, and the Mission of God* (New York: Harper One, 2008), 208, emphasis added.
13. Ibid., 64.
14. Albert M. Wolters, *Creation Regained: Biblical Basics for a Reformational Worldview* (Grand Rapids, Mich.: Eerdmans, 1985), 61.
15. Harry Emerson Fosdick, "The Meaning of Prayer," in Rueben P. Job and Norman Shawchuck, eds., *A Guide to Prayer* (Nashville: Upper Room, 1983), 263.

Chapter 3

1. Walter Brueggemann, "2 Kings 5: Two Evangelists and a Saved Subject," *Missiology: An International Review* 35, no. 3 (July 2007): 266.
2. Rick Shenkman, *Just How Stupid Are We? Facing the Truth about the American Voter* (New York: Basic, 2008), 7.
3. Peter Strupp and Alan Dingman, *Fat, Dumb, and Ugly: The Decline of the Average American* (New York: Simon & Schuster, 2004), 48.
4. John Micklethwait and Adrian Wooldridge, *God Is Back: How the Global Revival of Faith Is Changing the World* (New York: Penguin, 2009), 132.
5. Timothy Garton Ash, *Free World: America, Europe, and the Surprising Future of the West* (New York: Random House, 2004), 90.
6. Don Cheadle and John Prendergast, *Not on Our Watch: The Mission to End Genocide in Darfur and Beyond* (New York: Hyperion, 2007), 87.
7. Ibid., 86.
8. R. Paul Stevens, *Seven Days of Faith: Every Day Alive with God* (Colorado Springs: NavPress, 2001), 38.
9. Mike Kaye, "The Tools of the Abolitionists," *www.bbc.co.uk/history/british/abolition/abolition_tools_gallery_07.shtml* (June 25, 2009).
10. Bob Goudzwaard, *Globalization and the Kingdom of God* (Grand Rapids, Mich.: Baker, 2001), 77.

11. Tim Sanders, *Saving the World at Work: What Companies and Individuals Can Do to Go Beyond Making a Profit to Making a Difference* (New York: Doubleday, 2008), 39.
12. Cheadle and Prendergast, *Not on Our Watch*, 180.
13. Ibid., 103.
14. Ibid., 235.
15. Robert F. Kennedy, "It Is from the Numberless" (address on the Day of Affirmation, University of Capetown, South Africa, June 6, 1966), quoted in Jeffery Sachs, *The End of Poverty: Economic Possibilities for Our Time* (New York: Penguin, 2005), 367–68.

Chapter 4

1. John Elkington, "Towards the Sustainable Corporation," *California Management Review* 36, no. 2 (1994): 90–100.
2. Michael Kinsley, *Creative Capitalism: A Conversation with Bill Gates, Warren Buffett and Other Economic Leaders* (New York: Simon & Schuster, 2008), 110.
3. "Cadbury Dairy Milk Commits to Going Fairtrade," March 4, 2009, *www.cadbury.com/media/press/Pages/cdmfairtrade.aspx* (accessed March 10, 2009).
4. Bill Gates, "A New Approach to Capitalism in the 21st Century" (speech, World Economic Forum 2008, Davos, Switzerland, January 24, 2008), *www.microsoft.com/presspass/exec/billg/speeches/2008/01–24WEFDavos.mspx* (August 18, 2009).
5. Tim Sanders, *Saving the World at Work: What Companies and Individuals Can Do to Go Beyond Making a Profit to Making a Difference* (New York: Doubleday, 2008), 62–63.
6. Ibid., 65.
7. Thich Nhat Hanh, *The Art of Power* (New York: HarperOne, 2007), 68.
8. Shane Claiborne, *Jesus for President: Politics for Ordinary Radicals* (Grand Rapids, Mich.: Zondervan, 2008), 243.
9. Ibid., 243.
10. Clive Mather, "Combining Principle with Profit: A Business Response to the Challenges of Globalization," in Peter Heslam, ed., *Globalization and the Good* (London: SPCK, 2004), 28.
11. Ibid., 36–37.
12. World Water Week, "About TapDC," *www.tapdc.org* (May 20, 2009).
13. Cheryl Tay, Mina Westman, and Audrey Chia, "Antecedents and Consequences of Cultural Intelligence among Short-Term Business Travelers," in *Handbook of Cultural Intelligence: Theory, Measurement, and Applications* (Armonk, N.Y.: M.E. Sharpe, 2008), 130.
14. David Livermore, *Leading with Cultural Intelligence* (New York: AMACOM, 2009), 185–86.

15. Sanders, *Saving the World at Work*, 95–97.
16. Kinsley, *Creative Capitalism*, 187.

Chapter 5

1. Jeffery Sachs, *The End of Poverty: Economic Possibilities for Our Time* (New York: Penguin, 2005), 366–67.
2. Max L. Stackhouse, Tim Dearborn, and Scott Paeth, *The Local Church in a Global Era: Reflections for a New Century* (Eugene, Ore.: Wipf and Stock, 2000), 103.
3. Gregg Easterbrook, *The Progress Paradox* (New York: Random House, 2004), 308.
4. Ibid.
5. Mark Noll, *The Scandal of the Evangelical Mind* (Grand Rapids, Mich.: Eerdmans, 1994), 206.
6. Brian J. Walsh and J. Richard Middleton, *The Transforming Vision: Shaping a Christian World View* (Downers Grove, Ill.: InterVarsity Press, 1984), 176.
7. Gregg Easterbrook, "The Forgotten Benefactor of Humanity," *Atlantic Monthly* (January 1999), *www.theatlantic.com/doc/199901/green-revolution*.
8. Tracy Kidder, *Mountains beyond Mountains: The Quest of Dr. Paul Farmer, a Man Who Would Cure the World* (New York: Random House, 2004).
9. Michael Kinsley, *Creative Capitalism: A Conversation with Bill Gates, Warren Buffett and Other Economic Leaders* (New York: Simon & Schuster, 2008), 13.
10. Muhammad Yunnus, *Banker to the Poor* (New York: Public Affairs, 2003), 47.
11. Shane Claiborne, *Jesus for President: Politics for Ordinary Radicals* (Grand Rapids, Mich.: Zondervan, 2008), 242.
12. Engineers Without Borders USA, "Featured Chapter: NY Professionals, Channeling the Rains to Feed 9,000," *www.ewb-usa.org/Chapters/FeaturedChapter/tabid/70/Default.aspx*.
13. Vestergaard Frandsen: Disease Control Textiles, "LifeStraw®," *www.vestergaard-frandsen.com/lifestraw.htm*.
14. Stackhouse et al., *The Local Church in a Global Era*, 98.
15. *www.thecommon.org/who* (June 25, 2009).
16. One Laptop per Child, "Laptop," *www.laptop.org/en/laptop/index.shtml* (June 15, 2009).
17. Ronald Cole-Turner, "Science, Technology, and Mission," in Stackhouse et al., *The Local Church in a Global Era*, 103.
18. Stackhouse et al., *The Local Church in a Global Era*, 98.

Chapter 6

1. Karl Paulnack, "The Value of Music" (welcome address), Mankato Symphony, *www.mankatosymphony.com/inspirationspeech(new).php.*
2. Ibid.
3. Ibid.
4. Rob Bell, *Drops Like Stars* (Grand Rapids, Mich.: Zondervan, 2009), 35–36.
5. Brad Pitt (interview with Diane Sawyer, ABC News, *Primetime Live*, New York, June 7, 2005).
6. John Micklethwait and Adrian Wooldridge, *God Is Back: How the Global Revival of Faith Is Changing the World* (New York: Penguin, 2009), 355.
7. Andy Crouch, *Culture Making: Recovering Our Creative Calling* (Downers Grove, Ill.: InterVarsity Press, 2008), 67–69.
8. "Interviews: Into the Fray," *Christianity Today, www.christianitytoday.com/music/interviews/2006/thefray–0706.html.*
9. UNHCR: The UN Refugee Agency, "News: Ben Affleck Video Unveiled for UNHCR Gimme Shelter Campaign," *www.unhcr.org/news/NEWS/4948ce084.html.*
10. Don Cheadle and John Prendergast, *Not on Our Watch: The Mission to End Genocide in Darfur and Beyond* (New York: Hyperion, 2007), 162.
11. Kids with Cameras, *www.kids-with-cameras.org/bornintobrothels/* (May 22, 2009).
12. Cheadle and Prendergast, *Not on Our Watch*, 141.
13. United Artists, "Hotel Rwanda," *www.unitedartists.com/hotelrwanda/main.html.*
14. Paulnack, "The Value of Music."
15. Stephen King, *On Writing: A Memoir of the Craft* (New York: Pocket, 2002), 270.

Chapter 7

1. Gregg Easterbrook, *The Progress Paradox* (New York: Random House, 2004), 46.
2. Franklin Payne, "The Goals of Medicine," *Journal of Biblical Ethics in Medicine* 5, no. 1 (2002): 20.
3. Lizette Larson-Miller, "Physician Intervention," *www.sfms.org/AM/Template.cfm?Section=Home&SECTION=Article_Archives&TEMPLATE=/CM/HTMLDisplay.cfm&CONTENTID=2332* (June 9, 2009).
4. American Psychological Association, "How Does Stress Affect Us?" APA Help Center, *http://helping.apa.org/work/stress2.html* (January 7, 2009).
5. P. Beitchman, "Mental and Physical Health: The Vital Connection," NAMI-NYC Metro, November 2002, *http://naminyc.nami.org/board_vitalconnection.htm.* (March 6, 2009).

6. William Easterly, *The White Man's Burden: Why the West's Efforts to Aid the Rest Have Done So Much Ill and So Little Good* (New York: Penguin, 2006), 249.
7. Ibid., 255.
8. Julie Walton, *www.calvin.edu/weblogs/pivot/more/some_foundational_thoughts_on_a_christian_philosophy/* (May 3, 2009).
9. *The Book of Common Prayer* (Cambridge: Oxford Univ. Press, 1979), 453.

Chapter 8

1. Shane Claiborne, *Jesus for President: Politics for Ordinary Radicals* (Grand Rapids, Mich.: Zondervan, 2008), 244, emphasis added.
2. "The National Entertainment State," *The Nation* (June 15, 2006), 72–73.
3. Greg Mortenson and David Oliver Relin, *Three Cups of Tea: One Man's Mission to Promote Peace ... One School at a Time* (New York: Penguin, 2006), 210.
4. Ibid., back cover.
5. Paulo Freire, *Pedagogy of the Oppressed* (New York: Continuum, 1997), 25.
6. Don Cheadle and John Prendergast, *Not on Our Watch: The Mission to End Genocide in Darfur and Beyond* (New York: Hyperion, 2007), 119.
7. Ibid., 162.

Chapter 9

1. This story and related study is more fully reported in my book *Cultural Intelligence: Improving Your CQ to Engage Our Multicultural World* (Grand Rapids, Mich.: Baker, 2009), 221–22.
2. William Easterly, *The White Man's Burden: Why the West's Efforts to Aid the Rest Have Done So Much Ill and So Little Good* (New York: Penguin, 2006), 382.
3. Andy Crouch, *Culture Making: Recovering Our Creative Calling* (Downers Grove, Ill.: InterVarsity Press, 2008), 189.
4. Nicholas D. Kristof, "Jobs for the Poor," *New York Times* (January 15, 2009), A10.
5. Ibid.
6. Soon Ang and Linn Van Dyne, "Conceptualization of Cultural Intelligence," in *Handbook of Cultural Intelligence: Theory, Measurement, and Applications* (Armonk, N.Y.: M.E. Sharpe, 2008), 3.
7. David Livermore, *Leading with Cultural Intelligence* (New York: AMACOM, 2009), 30–31.

Chapter 10

1. Popularized by Rick Warren, *The Purpose Driven Life: What on Earth Am I Here For?* (Grand Rapids, Mich.: Zondervan, 2002), 236.

2. Os Guinness, *The Call: Finding and Fulfilling the Central Purpose of Your Life* (Nashville: Word, 1998), 31, emphasis added.
3. Ibid.
4. Timothy Ferris, *The 4-Hour Workweek: Escape 9–5, Live Anywhere, and Join the New Rich* (New York: Crown, 2007), 273.
5. Richard Chang, *The Passion Plan: A Step-by-Step Guide to Discovering, Developing, and Living Your Passion* (San Francisco: Jossey-Bass, 2001), 150–52.
6. Parker Palmer, *Let Your Life Speak: Listening for the Voice of Vocation* (San Francisco: Jossey-Bass, 1999), 5.
7. Ibid., 16.
8. Portions of the "Personal Inventory" section are adapted from "How to Discover Your Passion," Debra Moorhead.com: *www.debramoorhead.com/blog/index.php/how-to-discover-your-passion/* (March 3, 2009).
9. Bill Hybels, *Holy Discontent: Fueling the Fire That Ignites Personal Vision* (Grand Rapids, Mich.: Zondervan, 2007).
10. Portions of this originally appeared in my book *Cultural Intelligence: Improving Your CQ to Engage Our Multicultural World* (Grand Rapids, Mich.: Baker, 2009), 125–26.
11. Palmer, *Let Your Life Speak,* 44.
12. "Shakertown Pledge," in Thomas G. Pettepiece, *Visions of a World Hungry,* quoted in Rueben Job and Norman Shawchuck, eds., *A Guide to Prayer for Ministers and Other Servants* (Nashville: Upper Room Books, 1985), 116–17.

Chapter 11

1. Bob Roberts Jr., *Glocalization: How Followers of Jesus Engage in a Flat World* (Grand Rapids, Mich.: Zondervan, 2007), 85.
2. William Schweiker, "The Church as an Academy of Justice: More Responsibility in the World of Mammon," in Max L. Stackhouse, Tim Dearborn, and Scott Paeth, eds., *The Local Church in a Global Era: Reflections for a New Century* (Grand Rapids: Eerdmans, 2000), 35–36.
3. Ruth Haley-Barton, *Sacred Rhythms: Arranging Our Lives for Spiritual Transformation* (Downers Grove, Ill.: InterVarsity Press, 2006), 182–85.
4. Mars Hill Bible Church, "Roots," *www.marshill.org/believe/directions/#* (August 18, 2009).
5. Bjorn Lomborg, "Lomborg Sets Global Priorites" (TED Talk, February 2005), *www.ted.com/talks/bjorn_lomborg_sets_global_priorities.html* (August 20, 2009).

Conclusion

1. Anthony Hoekema, *Created in God's Image* (Grand Rapids, Mich.: Eerdmans, 1986), 95.

2. Mary Forman, *Praying with the Desert Mothers* (Collegeville, Minn.: Liturgical Press, 2005), 37.

FAQs

1. John R. W. Stott, *Christian Mission in the Modern World* (Downers Grove, Ill.: InterVaristy Press, 1975), 31.
2. Os Guinness, *The Call: Finding and Fulfilling the Central Purpose of Your Life* (Nashville: Word, 1998), 34.
3. Cornelius Plantinga, *Engaging God's World: A Christian Vision of Faith, Learning, and Living* (Grand Rapids, Mich.: Eerdmans, 2002), 111.
4. Bill O'Reilly, "How Can You Cut through That?" *The O'Reilly Factor*, Fox News (September 1, 2004).
5. Ibid.
6. William Easterly, *The White Man's Burden: Why the West's Efforts to Aid the Rest Have Done So Much Ill and So Little Good* (New York: Penguin, 2006), 115.

Global Youth Ministry

Reaching Adolescents Around the World

Terry Linhart and David Livermore, General Editors

As the world's youth population continues to grow and interact globally, youth ministry is developing in equal fashion. Local fellowship and growth is mingled with international blogging, texting, and electronic socializing. Global youth ministry presents enormous opportunities, but it also requires the careful education and preparation of youth leaders.

Seeking to write a definitive yet succinct textbook on the challenges and requirements of international ministry, authors Terry Linhart and David Livermore invited twenty-three prominent youth ministry leaders from around the world to contribute chapters. The overarching purpose was to focus on essential topics and to inform readers on the various theological, theoretical, sociocultural, and historical issues that shape international youth ministry.

Global Youth Ministry uses diverse voices from mainline, evangelical, and Catholic ministries to bridge international and denominational divisions and ensure there's no agenda from a particular theological or political niche. The result is a useful and versatile text that both challenges and educates ministry students with a heart for missions and a spiritual empathy for youth around the world.

Available in stores and online!

Share Your Thoughts

With the Author: Your comments will be forwarded to the author when you send them to *zauthor@zondervan.com.*

With Zondervan: Submit your review of this book by writing to *zreview@zondervan.com.*

Free Online Resources at

www.zondervan.com

Zondervan AuthorTracker: Be notified whenever your favorite authors publish new books, go on tour, or post an update about what's happening in their lives at www.zondervan.com/authortracker.

Daily Bible Verses and Devotions: Enrich your life with daily Bible verses or devotions that help you start every morning focused on God. Visit www.zondervan.com/newsletters.

Free Email Publications: Sign up for newsletters on Christian living, academic resources, church ministry, fiction, children's resources, and more. Visit www.zondervan.com/newsletters.

Zondervan Bible Search: Find and compare Bible passages in a variety of translations at www.zondervanbiblesearch.com.

Other Benefits: Register yourself to receive online benefits like coupons and special offers, or to participate in research.